BREAK-OUT!

*Dramatic, real-life escape stories
that read like fiction.*

D1198728

PHOTO: COLM HOGAN

Paddy Hayes is a writer and film-maker with his own production company, Flutterby Films, based in Galway. Most of his work is made for TG4, Irish-language TV, for whom his latest venture is a six-part series based on the escapes covered in this book. He has previously worked for the Irish Film Board and lectures in scriptwriting in the National University of Ireland, Galway.

Roger M Schlosser
2010

Break Out!

FAMOUS PRISON ESCAPES

PADDY HAYES

THE O'BRIEN PRESS
DUBLIN

First published 2004 by The O'Brien Press Ltd,
20 Victoria Road, Dublin 6, Ireland.
Tel: +353 1 4923333; Fax: +353 1 4922777
E-mail: books@obrien.ie
Website: www.obrien.ie
Reprinted 2004.

ISBN: 0-86278-875-7

Text © copyright Paddy Hayes 2004
Copyright for typesetting, layout, editing, design
© The O'Brien Press Ltd

All rights reserved. No part of this publication may be reproduced
or utilised in any form or by any means, electronic or mechanical,
including photocopying, recording or by any information storage and
retrieval system, without permission in writing from the publisher.

British Library Cataloguing-in-Publication Data
Hayes, Paddy
Break-out! : famous prison escapes
1.Escapes - Ireland - History - 20th century
2.Escapes - Northern Ireland - History - 20th century
I.Title
365.6'41

2 3 4 5 6 7 8 9 10
04 05 06 07 08 09 10

COVER PICTURES: (front) *top and bottom* Flutterby Films,
top right Derry escapee Rocky Burns, photo courtesy of the Burns family;
(back) handbill widely distributed by the security
forces after the escape from the Maze.
Every effort has been made to trace copyright holders of photographs
used in the book, but if any infringement has occurred
the publishers request the holders of such copyright to contact them.

Layout, typesetting, editing and design: The O'Brien Press Ltd
Printing: Nørhaven Paperback A/S

CONTENTS

For Noelle

INTRODUCTION

The need to escape has existed since men began capturing and imprisoning one another. Since tribal battles in primitive times, enemy forces have been taken prisoner and held in captivity, whether as hostages, as slaves, or to be punished in defeat by torture and execution. In such a position, often a life-or-death situation, the prisoner immediately turns his thoughts to escaping; outwitting his captors, overpowering his guards, and overcoming the obstacles set against him. It requires careful planning and preparation, as breaking free from the shackles means nothing if one is caught immediately afterwards and returned to prison, usually to face a jailer even more watchful and determined than before.

As important as the break-out itself is the successful getaway. Especially in wartime, the high point is returning to one's own people in triumph, thereby humiliating one's enemies. Otherwise the escape is in vain.

This triumphant return has often been exploited by republican organisations for propaganda purposes, and it was not uncommon for IRA escapees to hold a press conference, usually at a secret location south of the border, less than a week after a successful break-out. In this way it could play an important political role, emphasising their status as prisoners of war and creating a wealth of rebellious, inspirational folklore for future members to draw from. It therefore meant much more than simply returning volunteers to active service. In fact, escapees were often a considerable

drain on the organisation when one considers the amount of support required to keep a fugitive in hiding.

In this book I have deliberately chosen escapes which are tribal
in nature, in that those participating were members of a tightly knit
group with quasi-military structures and strictly defined principles.
Four of the stories involve republicans, whilst the other two are of
spies caught behind enemy lines in Ireland.

While there have been many civilian escapes, they possess little
of the intrigue which is present in escapes of a political nature.
Invariably, ODC (ordinary decent criminal) escapees lack the guile
to evade recapture, or the organisational structures to shelter them,
and have no particular motive in escaping other than self-interest.
More often than not, criminal escapees are recaptured when they
return home to visit family and friends.

By contrast, republican attitudes towards escape were largely
conditioned by their view of themselves as soldiers, and their ability to see their incarceration, not only in personal, but in political
and symbolic terms. Simply put, republicans viewed their own
captivity as akin to that of their country, and believed that by
escaping they were striking a blow for Irish freedom. It was a delib-
erate affront to the authorities' power, teaching them a crucial
lesson about the nature of resistance. It was not simply to get prisoners out: in fact, republicans were not permitted to abscond while
on home leave and you could have the bizarre situation where a
prisoner would return to prison from home leave while actively
engaged in an escape plan.

Seeing themselves as prisoners of war, the republicans ironically
drew inspiration from the escapes effected by British POWs in Nazi
camps during World War II, so much so that they often referred to
the warders as the 'Germans'. This, along with the rich tradition of
escape stories by past IRA men, served as a morale booster, to help
resist the debilitating effects of being held in captivity, a psychological defeatism the US military calls 'barbed-wire syndrome'. The

possibility of escape, even in the most extreme of conditions, instilled an *esprit de corps* in the prisoners, and gave hope to those facing enormously long sentences, or interned indefinitely without trial.

The two non-republican escapes in the book have one thing in common: they were both carried out by spies involved at varying levels with republican organisations. In common with republicans, espionage agents would be trained and detailed to escape from custody if captured. In addition, these spies were engaged behind enemy lines and were often in real physical danger, so their escapes were motivated by the same sense of urgency which characterises republican ones.

This book is not intended as an exhaustive account of Irish escapes. As there were over eighty successful escapes by republicans alone in the twentieth century, such a volume would run to thousands of pages. I have limited my focus to those that are still within living memory, and possess intriguing features unique to themselves. There is a fascination with escapes in the modern psyche, a factor which explains the success of such films as *The Shawshank Redemption*, *Papillon*, *Escape from Alcatraz*, *The Great Escape*, and many more. They contain the perpetually appealing tale of the little guy using his intelligence, guile, and considerable courage to overcome seemingly insurmountable obstacles and emerge free and victorious in the end. Whether you consider the republicans murderers or political prisoners; whether you consider the spies perfidious knaves or heroic intelligence agents; there is nonetheless a sneaking regard for their ability to beat the system. Everyone loves an escapee ...

Just a Girl

SHE SAT ON TOP OF MOUNTJOY PRISON'S OUTER WALL, urging her companion to grasp the homemade rope ladder which was dangling into the exercise yard. A searchlight swung around to pick out her silhouette. As the light hit her, so did the realisation that she had to abandon her companion and go it alone. She could easily be shot. She threw her bags to the ground below, and prepared to jump. The wall was three times her height. She sailed through the air and rolled awkwardly as she landed. Luckily she was wearing her flat shoes. Her husky voice groaned with pain as she put weight on her sprained ankle and tottered off down the canal as quickly as her injury would allow her. As she rounded a corner, a dog growled in a back yard and startled her, but she stumbled determinedly onwards, hugging the shadows. The streets were menacingly quiet during the Emergency, as World War II was called in Ireland. Arriving at a house, she knocked urgently at the door in a panic. As it opened, the lamplight fell onto her face, revealing that her lipstick was running and her headscarf was askew. But this was no lady. This was a man in drag. This frantic stranger at the door was the German spy, Gunter Schutz.

In today's Silesia in southern Poland, you will hear little German spoken, yet this is where Gunter Schutz wailed his way into the world on 16 June 1912, in the town of Schweidniz. His early years were marked by the absence of his father Max who, during the Great War that the whole world thought would be the last, worked as an engineering station commander in France. Gunter grew up in the far-eastern reaches of a Germany where the national defeat in the Great War and the Treaty of Versailles were bitterly resented. As a young boy he would run from his house to join the neighbours gazing upwards for a glimpse of the Red Baron, Manfred von Richthofen, who was famed for his audacious exploits in the war. In Silesia the Baron was a local hero, and would often be seen performing aerial stunts for his adoring young fans. Recognising his home-town, he would dip his wings in salute. As Gunter waved skyward in delight he could hardly have imagined that his fatherland would one day, in the second war to end all wars, dispatch him in a fighter plane to Ireland as a spy.

Although Schweidniz was predominantly Catholic, the Schutzes were members of the Protestant minority and Gunter attended the local Protestant school. Sometimes, on his way home after school, Gunter would wander down Schweidniz's main street, where there was a wonderland of magic and colour to be found in the toy shop. A gaunt, grey-haired old Jew with a triangular goatee and kind eyes, the shopkeeper made many of the toys himself. The young Gunter must have marvelled at the model soldiers and tin drums that decorated the musty walls and, holding one of the toy soldiers in his little hand, dreamed of joining the army some day.

BREAK-OUT!

Just before he was to be dispatched to Ireland in 1941, Gunter bumped into the toy seller on the street and greeted him fondly. The man motioned with his eyes as if to say: Be careful, you should not be speaking to a Jew. For the first time, Gunter felt discomfort at the extent to which the Nazi party was interfering in the lives of ordinary people. This ambivalence was to stick with him as he fought for the country he loved, run by a man he despised.

▲ ▲ ▲

Heavy snowfall brought Gunter and his pals clambering up to the top of the Sudeten mountains that bordered Czechoslovakia to the south. However, this was not the pleasurable experience known to skiers today, for in 1930s Silesia ski lifts were a thing of the future, and so Gunter and his mates had to hike their way to the summit, carrying their skis on their backs. Though an arduous task, their youthful fitness and the promise of a veritable paradise on the other side of the mountain where the Czech *frauleins* would greet them with open arms and fluttering hearts, drove them on. When they reached the summit, they hurriedly donned their skis and hit the slopes with wild abandon, chasing each other down the mountainside and boasting of triumphs to come that evening. To the Czechs, these visitors from the north were exotic and free, and this is where Gunter got a taste for the philandering lifestyle that he would later enjoy. Though he did not yet have the money or the lifestyle that accompanied it, he quickly learned how to be a flash Harry in a foreign land.

As Gunter advanced into his twenties, his thoughts turned towards forming a more serious relationship and his eyes fell on Lilo Hienze, an eighteen-year-old beauty from his home-town. Although there were several years between them, they had quite a lot in common, and spent as much time in each other's company as possible.

But then, still in his twenties, Gunter made his way to London to study economics in a business college, where he obtained an enviable command of the language and mannerisms of the English. Around the same time he underwent his reserve-army training as a conscript in Germany, and a friend in the Abwehr (German military intelligence) introduced him to his boss, a Dr Scholl, who asked the young Gunter to do his duty by his country – to make casual observations whilst in Britain and report on military activity there. Gunter delivered the goods. On his return to Germany shortly after the outbreak of war, he was considered potentially useful to the Abwehr because of his international experience, and was transferred from his Oldenburg artillery regiment to the Abwehr in Hamburg. His ability to speak English, in actual fact, saved him from the grim fate of the rest of his unit, who were to freeze to death during Hitler's disastrous attack on Stalingrad. Instead, he was sent around mainland Europe where he was to investigate safe drops or mailboxes for the German military. Life as a courier for the intelligence services was a much more appealing proposition than one which led to a frozen grave on the eastern front. He stayed in lavish hotels as he flew from one European capital to another on a generous expense account, dined out almost every night, and generally relished *la dolce vita*. It was while staying at the Majestic hotel in German-friendly Barcelona that Gunter was instructed to write to various friendly contacts in Dublin, undercover agents whom the German command referred to as 'V' men.

This was his first indication that perhaps he was being groomed for a mission to Ireland. One of those friendly con-tacts was Werner Unland, a German married to an English woman, who lived in Dublin's Merrion Square. All four of Gunter's letters to Unland were surreptitiously opened by G2, Irish military intelligence, then cunningly re-sealed and forwarded. When Gunter was happy that he had laid some groundwork for the forthcoming mission he returned to Hamburg to his immediate boss, Captain Praetorious, who groomed these young recruits for the Abwehr. It was there that Praetorius told him to prepare for his Irish mission, and put him through his paces with a crash course in interna-tional spying. A fellow agent introduced him to the microdot system, a revolutionary new means of concealing data devel-oped by the Abwehr, and he was given lessons in meteorol-ogy, morse code, and radio transmission, all of which he was to use when reporting back to the German High Command. He memorised reams of code, such as 'Bulldog' for Britain, 'Mackerel' for Ireland, and 'Bullfrog' for Portugal. Finally, Praetorius handed him Charles Garvice's novel *Just a Girl*, which he was to use as a code when transmitting messages.

German military intelligence in Ireland, however, was something of a contradiction in terms. For example, while being briefed for his mission, Gunter was told that his fellow agent Hermann Goertz had been received as a liberator by the Irish, and was roaming unhindered around Dublin in full Nazi regalia. Little distinction was drawn between the Irish army and the IRA – as far as the Abwehr were concerned they were one and the same. Sure wasn't the leader De Valera a former IRA man? Gunter was instructed, on landing in Ireland, to make his way to Dublin where he was to follow up his contact with Werner Unland. To this end, he was given Unland's photograph and was told to introduce himself as a friend of 'Schmidt', and refer to the 'Majestic hotel'.

His primary mission in Ireland was to transmit weather reports to Germany, information that would aid German assaults on neighbouring Britain. He was also to make contact with the IRA, and hire agents in the Six Counties of Northern Ireland to investigate war activity there, such as the movement of troops. The Abwehr provided him with a doctored passport, that of a childhood friend from Silesia called Hans Marschner, who had been born in Leuederitzbucht, a former German colony in South Africa. It was thought that a South African would be better able to move about without arousing suspicion. Gunter's photograph was seamlessly inserted in Hans's place and the written details were changed to suit Gunter's – height 5ft 9in, eyes: brown.

At this stage of the war, Hitler's armies had overrun Poland, Holland, Belgium and France. To the north, Denmark and Norway had fallen to the Nazi advance. British cities were being bombed relentlessly, and the United States was maintaining its dignified neutrality. As far as Gunter was concerned his mission to Ireland was to be a brief one, as it was only a matter of time before Britain was to be brought to her knees, and *Deutschland* was once again über alles. Ironically, and rather naively, he looked forward to being reunited with the good friends he had made in London.

It was, therefore, a bold and confident Gunter who

BREAK-OUT!

embarked on his first real spying mission. On 12 March 1941, in Schipol airport, Amsterdam, Gunter boarded the *Heinkel III* aircraft with flying officer Edmund Gartenfeld. As they cruised over the English midlands, at an altitude of 16,000 feet and at a speed of 180 MPH (which was breakneck in those days), Gunter gazed absently out the window reflecting on what he had left behind, and wondered what his reception would be when he returned to his fiancée, Lilo, and his family. He was awakened from his reverie by a cold blue glow filling the cabin. The night sky, visible through the aircraft's window, lit up brilliantly. Could this be the Aurora Borealis? Outside, a blaze of anti-aircraft fire shot skywards, but always fell short. Though he was initially quaking in his boots, a reassuring glance from officer Gartenfeld assured him that their altitude was such that they could not be hit. Gunter relaxed enough to marvel at the bursting anti-aircraft shells through the fibreglass window. They were passed from one beam of light to another, so their journey across England was illuminated all the way, akin to a ballerina gliding across a stage. When, at length, the anti-aircraft fire and the search-lights were left behind them in the east, Gunter braced himself for the adventure that was about to commence.

His heart in his mouth and his briefcase clutched to his breast, he threw himself into the dark sky. This was his first ever parachute jump. Hurtling head-first through the dark air, Gunter initially had the strange sensation of rising heavenward – while he had heard of the sensation of ground rush, he now felt the opposite, a soaring upwards towards the stars, until he felt the violent tug on his shoulders of his parachute poofing into life and calming his descent. This was how Gunter entered the country he was eventually to make his home.

▲ ▲ ▲

In the townland of Ballycullane, County Wexford, a farmer, who was an early riser and often woke before the dawn, was out walking when he thought he heard a strange sound in the dark distance. Then a violent flap turned his attention heavenward, where he saw a man in a parachute falling through the early-morning sky.

He had followed the war closely on the wireless. A De Valera man to the core, he thought that staying neutral in the war was the only way this fledgling country could assert its independence from the empire. With Hitler advancing on Britain, this little corner of south-east Ireland suddenly took on a military significance. There was speculation in the village as to who would invade Ireland first, the Germans or the British, so he thought better of approaching this aerial visitor. He simply turned into his cottage and resolved to report the sighting to the Gardaí when he walked to town later that day.

A couple of hundred yards in front of the farmer's cottage, Gunter Schutz rolled as his feet hit the ground and the parachute enveloped him. He touched his nose to discover it was bleeding. He looked around at the dawn. He was now a spy.

Using the shovel he had carried with him, he dug a hole in the ground where he buried his Luftwaffe jacket and parachute and, as he believed he had landed outside Newbridge in County Kildare some thirty miles from Dublin, set off in what he thought was the direction of the city. Donning his English raincoat and carrying his briefcase, he was heading down a boreen when he encountered a young girl cycling a bicycle. He stood out like a *wienerschnitzel* in an Irish stew and didn't help matters by asking directions to a place that was actually over seventy-five miles away. Well, I wouldn't start from here, she must have thought as she directed him to the main road, where he encountered a signpost reading: New Ross, 10 miles – this was a fortuitous discovery as most signposts had been painted over to prevent just this type of knowledge getting into the wrong hands! He guessed that New Ross must be a suburb of Dublin, but after walking for some time and not having seen any indication of a large city approaching, he consulted his map and discovered just where New Ross lay relative to his destination. Obviously Gartenfeld's navigational skills were not blessed with Teutonic precision, and Gunter was lucky to have ended up on dry land at all!

It was not long before word reached the local constabulary of a stranger in their midst, and so two Gardaí were dispatched, on their trusty bicycles, in the direction of the reported encounters. They easily identified this handsome gent walking the roads as the man they were looking for. When stopped and asked his name and business, he replied, 'My name is Hans Marschner, my car has broken down – I am looking for a mechanic.' 'Do you mind if we have a look inside your case?' asked one of the Gardaí. On inspection it burst open and out spilled the radio transmitter, the real and forged bank notes, and a powerful microscope. Gunter claimed to be a philatelist and that the microscope was for his extensive stamp collection. 'Oh right, stamp collecting, is it?' murmured one of the Gardaí as Gunter was led back to the village of Taghmon from whence he had just come.

'What will happen to me?' he inquired anxiously. 'I suppose they'll string you up,' came the reply, and the two Gardaí guffawed. In Cullen's pub on the main street, the Gardaí used their most potent counter-espionage weapon as they awaited the arrival of Branchmen from Dublin. They plied their German visitor full of porter.

Taken to the Bridewell Interrogation Centre for questioning by G2, Gunter was asked to write down a few words, which agents were able to identify as being by the same hand that had written the intercepted letters sent to Unland by a certain Gunter Schutz. However, the authorities did not disclose this knowledge, and continued to call him Marschner for the duration of the war. They inquired as to why he had a number of magazine cuttings on him containing advertisements for Aspro and the Green Park hotel. The innocuous little O in Aspro contained the revolutionary microdot system, within which was concealed up to thirty typewritten pages of text. Magnified four hundred times with a microscope such as Gunter's, it contained vital information such as top secret addresses in Ireland, code words, names, telephone numbers and addresses of Irish contacts. The Abwehr were so certain that this means of concealment would not be discovered that the contents were not even written in code. However, G2 quickly made the connection between the microscope and the mysterious advertisements, and were able to decipher Gunter's instructions all too easily.

At this stage, Gunter's mission seemed hopeless – he had been picked up within hours of arrival and within a day the authorities had discovered his secret mission. But consolation must have come from the fact that none of the other German spies had been at liberty for terribly long either. 'Dad's Army' could have run a better spy ring, as they were quite the ragbag of operatives and obviously did not represent the Reich's best and most efficient. The most colourful character was Ernst Weber-Drohl, who had fought as a wrestler under the name of 'Atlas the Strong' and was famed for lifting a platform holding twelve people over his head. He was sent by U-boat, at the ripe old age of sixty, to land in Ireland and make surreptitious contact with the IRA. When he was arrested in 1940 for illegally entering Ireland, he freely admitted that he had done so, but maintained that he was acting with the best of intentions. He claimed that when he toured Ireland thirty-three years previously as 'Atlas the Strong', he had fathered two sons whom he now hoped to track down. His story was deemed too outrageous to be fabricated and his internment lasted a mere week in 1940, although he was re-interned in 1942.

Jan Van Loon was a keen supporter of Dutch National Socialism and was therefore reluctantly fighting on the side of the Allies in the Dutch navy. He was stationed in Northern Ireland when Germany declared war on communist Russia in 1941, and he felt so compelled to switch sides in the conflict that he tried to make his way back, to fight for the Reich, via the German embassy in neutral Dublin. The Special Branch were, of course, watching all visitors to the embassy, and when they found him with incriminating British military drawings he was sent to Mountjoy as a spy.

Willy Preetz, who was married to a girl from Tuam, had a forged Irish passport under the name of Paddy Mitchell even before the outbreak of hostilities. Back in Germany the authorities recognised his initiative, and his predilection for assuming false identities, and gave him an assignment in Ireland. His integration skills were obviously superior to those of his fellow German operatives, especially as he had acquired a convincing Irish accent, and with the help of forged bank notes he was able to rent a small shop in Dublin city. From there he sent messages to the fatherland, using his Abwehr issued transmitter, until he was arrested. It is not known who betrayed him, but the authorities got a tip-off about his activities and he too was interned in Mountjoy.

The unfortunate Werner Unland was interned on evidence that the authorities discovered on Gunter's person. Henry Obed, a Muslim born in Lucknow, India, and two German South Africans, Dieter Gartner and Herbert Tributh, simply couldn't integrate seamlessly into the Cork community and were quickly arrested. In their possession the Special Branch found tins of French peas packed with explosives, as well as hollowed-out blocks of wood containing detonators and leather belts concealing lengths of safety fuse and slabs of nitro-cellulose. Through interrogation G2 discovered that their mission was to make their way to London and blow up Buckingham Palace. Whilst masquerading as a Swede living in Australia, Walter Simon was apprehended when he fell foul of the demon drink and spoke indiscreetly to detectives whom he met on the Killarney train. These spies' lack of vigilance was matched only by their ineptitude, the exception being Herman Goertz, who remained at liberty in Ireland from 5 May 1940 to the end of 1941.

Born into privilege and fanatically anti-communist, Goertz was an enthusiastic supporter of the Nazis and spent the late

BREAK-OUT!

1930s spying on the RAF on their behalf. When he returned to Germany, he was asked if he was interested in kindling a republican rebellion against the British in the Six Counties of Northern Ireland. He consulted widely on Irish political affairs, and among those from whom he sought advice was the lecturer in Anglo-Irish literature in Berlin University, Francis Stuart, to whose wife's house in Wicklow Goertz made his way when he parachuted into Ireland. He was a competent agent but he was constantly frustrated by the IRA's lack of organisation, and it was he who famously stated that the IRA knew how to die for its country but not how to fight for it. After a year and a half of clandestine activity he was picked up whilst in a safe house and interned.

▲▲▲

The German internees in Mountjoy were housed in the jail's hospital wing by the Royal canal, and were isolated from the three hundred IRA internees as well as the ordinary criminals. In wartime the prison was under armed military guard, and escape was considered extremely unlikely, if not impossible. Daytime escape was impractical as the sentries had an elevated view of both sides of the exterior wall from their posts, and by night they patrolled the grounds on foot. Whilst in Mountjoy, Gunter made good friends with the Dutchman Van Loon, and their thoughts turned to making an escape bid. The two of them had adjoining cells on the ground floor, and Van Loon soon discovered that he was able to lift the floorboards beneath his bed. The plan was to dig deep enough to get below the foundations, and then to burrow a tunnel to the other side of the exterior wall, and ultimately to liberty.

By night, as all lay sleeping, the painstaking digging commenced and progress was good. Van Loon's bed was occupied with a dummy made of clothes to avoid arousing suspicion when the warder came around on patrol and observed the cell through a peephole. A signalling system was required to stop Van Loon digging when the warder approached, as the noise he made could be heard from the corridor outside. The two managed to scrape an opening beside a heating pipe that went between their rooms and pass a string through. If Gunter heard the warder approaching he would tug on the string, which was wrapped around Van Loon's neck as he worked. A quick tug would be enough to stop the noise of scraping until the warder passed, and then excavation would commence again, into an ever-deepening hole. Working through the night meant a lack of sleep for the two, which left them groggy and irascible during the day. However, the progress in the digging was ample compensation for this, as the hole was not long in reaching the bottom of the exterior wall. During their daytime strolls around the grounds they would nonchalantly release the clay and stones, which they had concealed in the legs of their trousers, into the shrubbery around the yard. In fact, work on the hole was proceeding so rapidly that they were finding it difficult to dispatch the amounts of clay they produced.

Gunter was nearly out of his mind with impatience. The four walls of his cell seemed to be closing in on him and he was perpetually exhausted. He closed his eyes so that the feeling might go away, but the walls seemed to encroach even quicker. Whilst Van Loon was digging, Gunter had to keep moving about to stop himself from falling asleep, as this would certainly lead to their plan being discovered. He lay on his bed, his ears perked for the warder whilst he listened to the relentless digging in the next cell, aware that Van Loon was tantalisingly close, and desperate for word of success.

When a tug on the string came from Van Loon, Gunter was sure that they had made a breakthrough. He leaned closer to the gap in the wall. 'I've hit a pool of water,' whispered Van Loon. 'Keep going,' said Gunter, 'there's bound to be water at that depth.' The following night, as Van Loon set to work, he noticed that more than just a pool of water had formed where he was digging, but he persevered. After three nights, disaster struck – the pool had developed into a flood, which made any further digging impossible. The Royal canal was likely to come in on top of them. They had been so close, but were now further than ever from liberty.

After this bitter disappointment they spent their time conceiving other means of escape. 'What if…' one would begin, but would trail off as he realised where his plan would be foiled. And so Gunter Schutz languished in Mountjoy and could only dream of returning to his native Germany. He feared for his family, and his beloved Lilo, who were exposed to dreadful peril. His father, Max, was sliding into ill health. (He was to die in 1943 without having seen his son in over four years.) As for Van Loon, he knew that if deported back to Holland he would certainly be executed for treason. For him, escape was a matter of life and death.

Just prior to Christmas, on 19 December 1941, the bell over the prison gate rang out to announce the death by hanging of the convicted murderer Patrick Kelly, and a note was pinned to the main gate declaring that the sentence of the law had been carried out. As each toll of the bell reverberated in his ears, Gunter imagined Kelly's last moments. A white noose would be draped over his head, his arms would be pinioned together with leather straps, and his legs, similarly strapped together, would stand gingerly on the large trapdoors on the floor. Albert Pierrepoint, the legendary British hangman, would be standing poised at the trapdoor lever. Once the lever was pulled, the trapdoors would fall away from under the condemned man, there would be a sudden snap, and there he would hang, lifeless. A shiver ran down Gunter's spine as the last bell pealed. The internees had been told that Pierrepoint's last job was to hang a German spy in England by the name of Richter. Gunter had trained with this very same Richter in the Abwehr, and recurring nightmares reminded him that this fate could easily be his. But recurring dreams also reminded him of the thrill of adventure that escape could bring.

Gunter had a great admiration for English culture and frequently requested Shakespeare and other literary tomes, which were delivered to the prison from Eason's bookshop. The wireless told of the Americans entering the war, yet the other German internees were still confident of a German victory and they mistrusted Gunter, who insisted on listening to the British stations on the wireless. He himself was homesick and he found many of his fellow Germans were fanatical Nazis, as well as being boorish and uncouth. He even suspected that Willy Preetz had stolen his watch. They, not entirely unsurprisingly, thought him snobbish, pro-British and soft-centred. Herman Goertz, in particular, believed Gunter to be a traitor and a coward who had disclosed too much information to the authorities on his arrest. As the information that had been seized from Gunter contained lists of top-secret addresses, which no doubt included the names of safe houses such as the one in which Goertz was arrested, perhaps his animosity was not entirely misplaced. He was a constant thorn in Gunter's side and took every available opportunity to display his hostility toward him. This served only to increase Gunter's appetite for escape, and he knew that as he could not rely on his fellow Germans, he would somehow have to get help from the IRA internees.

▲▲▲

One day while exercising in the grounds of the hospital wing, Gunter spotted a wiry young Irishman strolling about, keeping his eyes fixed on his shoes. It was unusual to see an Irish prisoner as the authorities purposely kept them and the Germans apart. Having made the acquaintance of Jim O'Hanlon, Gunter discovered him to be a tempestuous IRA member who had fallen foul of the organisation's commanding officer in the jail and was being subjected to three days' ostracisation. As a result, Governor Sean Kavanagh had granted his request to exercise apart from his comrades in the hospital grounds. This young man proved to have a loquacious manner and numerous contacts on the outside. He supplied Gunter with a detailed map of the vicinity of the prison, as well as addresses for a number of safe houses that would harbour any enemy of the oldest adversary of them all, the Brits. Gunter was now better prepared for a life on the outside, thanks to this young IRA volunteer, than he had been by German military intelligence. Equally useful to Gunter, this young volunteer gave him a crash course in Irish history and the progress of the Irish Republican Army. All Gunter lacked was the means to get outside.

The Germans in Mountjoy were subject to fewer restrictions than their IRA counterparts. They were afforded free association by day, and Gunter was at sufficient liberty to play a game of chess with one of the warders. 'Check,' said the warder as he advanced a second rook to a strong line of attack. He was a superior chess player and it was not long before Gunter was hoodwinked into a checkmate. Gunter was to achieve the greater hoodwink, however. He innocently ordered a woman's fur coat, cosmetics, and some flat plimsolls from the prison authorities. Needless to say, he was soon summoned to the Governor's office. Governor Kavanagh was understandably suspicious of his intentions, but Gunter explained that quality clothes, and other such luxuries, had become scarce in war-time Germany and were a gift for his fiancée back home. Kavanagh checked the size of the shoes on order and compared it to Gunter's own. The women's shoes were size five and a half (the equivalent of a German thirty-eight) and Gunter wore a forty-one. The governor stamped his approval on the request. This was far too easy, Gunter thought to himself.

As Christmas approached, Governor Kavanagh announced that a variety show was to be performed in the prison workshop for all the inmates, and their relatives were to be invited. Back home Gunter had always dressed up for the theatre, but this time he donned two sets of clothes. Snakelike, he would dispense with his outward male layer during the performance, don his headscarf and fur coat, and make his way out with the visiting relatives dressed as a woman. Because of the festivities the warders' vigilance was relaxed somewhat, and towards the end of the show Gunter made his way unnoticed into the Gents. He was soon to discover that a warder had stationed himself just outside the toilet door and would certainly see through his disguise. He waited as long as he could, hoping that the warder would disappear, but it was in vain. Eventually he returned to his seat dejectedly, and clapped lamely as the ecstatic actors on stage took their bows.

After this incident he realised that a solo escape bid was a non-starter, and that he would need further help and co-operation. The only place where Gunter was able to associate freely with non-German prisoners was the infirmary waiting room. He used any excuse to go to the doctor and his illnesses became legendary among the other internees. There Gunter met an ordinary prisoner, 'Johnny the Englishman', who worked there as an attendant and who informed him that he could obtain the means to escape for a price. On a subsequent visit, 'Johnny the Englishman' slipped Gunter a flat object wrapped in paper. Gunter's heart leapt with exhilaration, and he tried to conceal the elation that shone in his eyes. On returning to his cell, Gunter unwrapped the paper to discover two old hacksaw blades. They were rusted and blunt but they were, nonetheless, effective. He now had the means to escape.

Gunter's stomach cramps and phantom illnesses escalated into vomiting fits and diarrhoea, as he frequently locked himself into one of the toilets that had three steel bars in the window. After informing his partner in crime Van Loon, he set about his sawing with excitement and determination. The noise of steel on steel was hideously grating and he had to quell his impatience, smearing the blade with soap to smother the sound somewhat. The work was as painstaking as the digging in Van Loon's cell and it took the two of them, working in relays, six weeks to finally saw through one inch of metal, but time was one thing that they had in abundance. Once they had cut right through the bar, repeated kicking and hitting brought it loose and there was enough room for a man to squeeze through. They replaced the bar and set about their plans. It was a seven-foot drop to the outside. Now their only obstacle was the perimeter wall, which was a daunting twenty-three feet high.

In a disused section of the hospital wing, the two discon-nected a water tap and broke off a thin twenty-foot section of piping. They connected this to a second and stronger piece of piping which, with a little cajoling by a blunt instrument, they managed to bend into a crook shape, much like a walking stick. The idea was that they would use the thin piece of piping to lever the stronger 'hooked' piece onto the top of the perimeter wall. To the other end of this they attached a rope they had manufactured from curtain material Gunter had ordered for his return to Germany. They were now ready; all they needed was the right time.

Back in the infirmary Gunter again met Jim O'Hanlon, whose family lived on Inisfallen Parade, a street which ran adjacent to the eastern wall of the prison. On his advice, Gunter had written on a piece of paper the addresses of numerous safe houses in the vicinity of the prison, which he planned to leave in his cell as a decoy. The O'Hanlons' address, however, he kept in his head.

Night had fallen over a smoggy Dublin on 28 February 1942, and a warder was whiling away the long Sunday evening in a game of cards with a German prisoner named Karl Anderson. Gunter had asked Anderson to occupy the warder's attention for as long as possible while he and Van Loon were making their escape bid. At about 9.30pm Gunter and Van Loon had stuffed clothes into their beds, just as they had done when Van Loon was digging. Under his overcoat, Gunter had donned his woman's clothing once more, and in the bathroom applied his make-up in front of the mirror, promising his reflection that this time his escape would be successful. He turned and gave Van Loon (who, incidentally, was not in drag) the same look. They removed the bar and lowered their escape accoutrements into the grounds below. They both jumped to the ground and rolled into the shadows as the spotlights swung above their heads. An armed sentry lit a cigarette and approached in their direction. They crouched low and held their breaths. Gunter felt that his heart must be booming like a kettledrum in the silent yard. The sentry then turned on his heel and continued on his round.

Meanwhile, back in the prison the warder tired of his game of cards and, despite Anderson's attempts to distract him, began his round of the cells. He noticed that all the prisoners were in their beds or otherwise accounted for. He then went to the toilet and discovered that it was locked from the inside. This was extremely suspicious as all the internees were supposedly elsewhere. He forced the door open and the gaping hole, where the bar once was, confronted him. As a chill gust of wind blew mockingly through his hair, an expression of disbelief crossed his face and he raised the alarm.

With the sentry out of sight, Gunter and Van Loon set about hoisting their contraption on to the perimeter wall. It connected on the first attempt, like a key slotting into a lock. Starting on Van Loon's shoulders, Gunter managed to haul himself up the curtain rope to the top of the wall. It was now Van Loon's turn. He dragged himself upwards, but each time his feet would not grip the curtain to give him any leverage. Gunter leaned downwards to drag him up but their hands would not connect. Suddenly, a spotlight as bright as day shone in their faces and the armed sentry came running towards them. It's now or never, thought Gunter and he simply rolled over the far side of the wall and landed with a thud and a stinging ankle. Their initial plan had been to use the contraption to scramble down the outside of the wall, but in the end the fall was no worse than his parachute landing in County Wexford.

He made his way to the house on Inisfallen Parade, where he was greeted as a friend by O'Hanlon's brother Joe, and his wife. They sprang into action in quasi-military fashion: Gunter's belongings were cast into a trapdoor hidden beneath the linoleum floor, and the women of the house re-applied Gunter's make-up and plonked a woman's hat on his head. They told him he was now 'only gorgeous'. His decoy seemed to be working, as the house was not one that was being searched. However, Joe O'Hanlon knew that it was only a matter of time before suspicion would fall on them, so he resolved to bring Gunter to his own house near Drumcondra, a mile or so away. Joe, his wife and Gunter set off hurriedly in that direction, and Gunter, despite the sprained ankle, was doing an impressive catwalk in his winter coat and elegant stockings. They turned a corner only to discover a roadblock erected by soldiers, obviously looking for him. Needless to say, Gunter had no papers. They were stopped when they reached the checkpoint and O'Hanlon was asked what his business was. 'The wife and I are escorting her sister home,' he replied. Gunter chose this moment to fix his suspenders, and the embarrassed soldiers averted their gaze, apologised for disturbing them and bade them on their way. As he minced away from them, Gunter made sure to waggle his bum as convincingly as possible while inside he was singing a song of freedom.

Joe O'Hanlon made contact with a strong republican matriarch, Caitlín Brugha, the widow of the former Minister of Defence, Cathal Brugha, and now a successful businesswoman running the Kingston Shirt Company. Caitlín arranged for Gunter to stay with an elderly couple by the name of Cowman, in Blackrock. Gunter's bus journey across the city dressed as a Dublin damsel passed without incident. It struck him as ironic that he had landed in this country with a copy of the novel *Just a Girl*, and here he was making his way around the city dressed in drag. To any passing spy-catcher he was indeed just a girl.

In Blackrock, he spent four days in the Cowmans' digs, where Mrs Brugha's daughters Neasa and Nóinín were also residing, but because it was a digs house, with lots of people coming and going, it was considered unsafe for Gunter to stay there for long. By now there were Wanted posters posted all over the city with his photograph and description on them, along with the promise of a reward of £500 for information leading to the capture of the fugitive. The whole situation was quite an embarrassment for De Valera's government, which was hedging its bets on the outcome of the war. Caitlín Brugha knew it was only a matter of time before his identity would be discovered, and so she arranged for him to hide out in her own house at Temple Gardens near Rathmines. This time Gunter made his way back across the city on a woman's bicycle, and as his dress fluttered in the breeze he relished the sense of excitement that the whole experience provided. It certainly beat being cooped up in Mountjoy! News of his escape reached Germany and he was promoted to the rank of lieutenant.

▲▲▲

At this time the IRA was in rag order. Internment on both sides of the border meant that the majority of activists were civic guests of the nation. De Valera, a former friend, had turned into an implacable foe and there were now no hiding places. Arrests, shootings and betrayals had left the IRA a beleaguered force. To a small group of activists at the top of Óglaigh na hÉireann in the North, such as Sean McCaughey, there appeared to be too many bungled operations and tip-offs to the authorities. They suspected that there was a traitor in their midst, and a process of elimination led them to the conclusion that it must be a southern senior-ranking officer. They believed that the then Chief of Staff, Stephen Hayes, had turned his coat and was feeding information on their operations to the Free State Special Branch. The only course of action open to the secret army was to arrest Hayes and execute him when he admitted his treason.

Hayes turned up for a routine IRA Army Council meeting in June 1941 only to discover that the ulterior motive of the meeting was to kidnap him and extract a confession. He was forcibly detained in various houses in Louth and Wicklow while a provisional army council was formed to decide on a course of action. Court-martialled on 23 July, with McCaughey as prosecutor, he was accused of conspiracy and treason; after ten hours the council returned a verdict of guilty on both counts and he was sentenced to death. Once sentenced, Hayes asked to be permitted to write a full and frank confession, and McCaughey and the council agreed to his request as it would explain his treachery to those who might still be faithful to their former commander.

The written confession was a lengthy document running to some one hundred and fifty pages and its composition took over two weeks. As the days passed, his captors became suspicious that Hayes was purposefully postponing his day of judgement. Was he just buying time? If he was, his tactic paid off as one night, when his guard was distracted, Hayes disarmed the guard, escaped through a window and made his way to the local Garda station, where he gave himself up. Hayes's and the IRA's accounts differ greatly on how the confession was extracted, and it has never been satisfactorily ascertained whether Hayes was actually a traitor or simply confessed because of torture. One thing that was certain, however, was that the IRA in the wake of the Hayes affair was a pretty bedraggled organisation.

In contrast, Caitlín's house, Ros na Ríogh, operated with admirable efficiency. There were trap doors and secret rooms where a fugitive could easily be concealed, and the house was frequently used for clandestine meetings of senior IRA members. Caitlín saw Gunter as a one-man liberation army, somebody who could give the IRA a badly needed shot in the arm with support and munitions from Germany. She organised for Gunter to meet with senior IRA staff, who devised a plan to sail him to occupied France where he could convince the German High Command to send arms and money. Bizarrely, he was asked to translate the Hayes confession into German and to take this to the High Command, as it was felt that it would strengthen their argument that German help was badly needed. He immediately set to work on translating the lengthy document, becoming more dubious of the organisation with each line he translated.

A small boat was purchased with the help of the German legation in Dublin and a swarthy, streetfighting sea-dog from Derry, called Charlie 'Nomad' McGuinness, was engaged to take Gunter to Brest in France. McGuinness was Ireland's greatest mercenary, whose adventurous life had taken him to fight on both sides of the Spanish civil war as well as on a polar expedition under Commander Byrd. In the early 1920s he had also helped the TD Bob Briscoe in a gun-running expedition from Germany, and was thus considered the right man for this operation.

On 30 April 1942, the boat was moored and ready in Bray, County Wicklow, and waiting for the car that was to pick him up that evening and bring him there filled Gunter with exhilaration. However, the authorities had been able to infiltrate what was a very leaky organisation and on the day they were to set sail, both Gunter and McGuinness were picked up by the Special Branch. The Branchmen arrived in Ros na Ríogh actually looking for McGuinness, but stumbled on Gunter who was reading on the veranda. 'Who are you?' asked one of the Branchmen. 'My name is Graves, from Sligo, I am just visiting here,' Gunter said. 'What's your address?' 'I live in Webster Gardens,' he replied, a former address in London which didn't sound like a credible address for somewhere so far from the Pale. This, coupled with his lack of a Sligo accent, aroused the Branchmen's suspicions and, drawing their revolvers, they ordered him to put his hands up. 'I'm the one you're looking for,' admitted Gunter, knowing now that the game was up and they had already identified him as the missing German spy whose description was on Wanted posters all over the city.

McGuinness was sentenced to seven years' imprisonment and Gunter was now in fear for his life. He was no longer the harmless and bungling secret agent who had parachuted into the arms of the Irish Special Branch, but a dangerous foreign national in league with an illegal underground organisation bent on the destruction of the state, and an escapee with a price on his head to boot. He was duly interrogated in the Bridewell Garda station for two days and then sent to Arbour Hill military prison for three months' solitary confinement. From there he was sent back to Mountjoy for a brief period before finally being sent to an internment camp in Athlone's Custume Barracks with his ten fellow German spies. Following Gunter's previous successful escape bid, the authorities thought it wiser to keep the German spies in isolation in rural Ireland as they were more conspicuous there.

With the war seeming to extend beyond what any of the

internees thought likely, tempers began to fray and in-fighting became rampant amongst them. Goertz was exasperated with Gunter for being weak under interrogation by the authorities when recaptured, and branded him a traitor. Goertz told Gunter that he would have him shot on their return to the fatherland. Van Loon was still hell-bent on an escape bid, and for once all the internees clubbed together in attempting another break for freedom. They manufactured a pulley system out of bed sheets to lift one of the huge stone slabs that made up the floor of the old cell, and Van Loon once again took up his old pastime of digging for his life.

They used every utensil they could manufacture to shift the earth and for a time a good deal of progress was being made by all the internees working together. Whilst some were digging, others spread the excess earth about the yard while the rest drowned out the noise by playing their mouth-organs. This seemed to concentrate their minds and the co-operation helped heal some of the rifts that had opened up between them. They only had to tunnel approximately thirty feet from the cell to the outside of the perimeter wall to freedom, and this time they did not encounter any water as they had done in Mountjoy. With their routine established, rapid progress was made on the tunnel and the plan seemed to be working. Then disaster struck one morning when an Irish corporal burst into Van Loon's cell as he lay in his bed and without a word went straight to the entrance of the tunnel. There was no doubt that somebody on the inside had tipped off the authorities. The long weeks of co-operative work had all been in vain. This incident, coupled with the increasingly depressing news from the war front, meant that tempers flared up and suspicions were cast about. The quarrelling started again.

Gunter now mistrusted his colleagues and soon laid plans to make a solo escape bid. He lay awake in his bed, and the familiar thoughts of the walls closing in on him returned. As he lay there, he absentmindedly fingered a hole in his mattress. While pulling at the contents, he noticed that a long mane of horse hair came loose in his hand. He sprang upright and pulled another clump of hair through. His penchant for dressing in drag returned to him as he draped it over his head and thought: This could make a very fine woman's wig. He set to work and, with some handy needlework, assembled his now-familiar escape costume. Besides the wig, he sewed together an attractive skirt from the lining of his overcoat, which was sufficiently long so that pinching shoes would not be required. He hid the costume in a bucket in one of the bathrooms, and bided his time for an opportunity to don the costume and make good his escape. But on the day he went to retrieve his costume, he discovered that one of his fellow internees had flushed most of it down the toilet, along with Gunter's dreams of escape. Who needs enemies, thought Gunter, and although he couldn't prove it, he was quite certain that Goertz was the culprit.

▲▲▲

With the United States now firmly behind the Allied war effort, Germany's retreat soon became a total collapse and the internees' thoughts turned to their own personal fate, rather than that of the fatherland. Of all the internees, Van Loon was the most endangered, as he was sure he would be hanged for treason if returned to his native Netherlands. He couldn't escape underground, but perhaps going in the opposite direction would yield results. With Goertz's aid he managed to saw a circular hole in the roof of the prisoner's mess, but the authorities discovered this, as usual, with suspicious ease.

During the summer of 1945 the two hundred or so German service personnel who had been interned in the Curragh camp were returned to Germany. In September, a government official visited the internees in Athlone, informed them that they were to be granted asylum in Ireland and that they were free to leave the camp until eleven each evening. Gunter was now able to visit the local hostelries and enjoy something of the life he had led before the war. As in his heyday in Czechoslovakia, the Germans aroused great interest among the local community and were fêted in each bar they went to. He could again be an exotic secret agent in a foreign land.

At a dance in St Mary's Hall he met Una Mackey, a nurse from Rathmines in Dublin who was on holidays in Athlone visiting her cousin. She was besotted with this exotic stranger. During the war she had been working in London's Paddington hospital when the bombs rained down in the Blitz, and she chided him for his war activity. This was Gunter's first encounter with Irish slagging. To a German this was a little puzzling but quite intriguing. Before long the Germans were released from the camp and Gunter resumed his acquaintance with Una in Dublin. On returning to civilian life in the capital, he proved to be quite an astute businessman and made good money re-selling disused British war materials. Obviously he had more flair for business than espionage! One of his most substantial deals was to sell disused cabling to the electricity board. By the spring of 1947 he was one of the few car owners in the capital, and his relationship with Una was blossoming. Post-war Germany was looking less and less attractive as a place to re-settle and Lilo had drifted out of his thoughts altogether.

On 12 April that year, early-morning visitors awakened the former German agents. They were arrested and taken to Mountjoy. The Allies wanted the German spies for questioning and De Valera, keen not to rock the boat further with the war victors, acquiesced. All the Germans fought their deportation orders in the courts and Goertz and Gunter were paroled to attend to personal matters. One rather pressing personal matter for Gunter was Una, and he asked her to marry him. As Gunter was a Protestant, the parish priest refused to marry them and suggested that Una should marry a nice Catholic. She protested to the Archbishop of Dublin, John Charles McQuaid, thinking that he, a more educated man, would see the humanity of the situation. The archbishop, however, was equally belligerent, and only when she threatened to marry in a registry office did he give his permission. However, as these mixed marriages could not be conducted in the full view of the faithful, it was to take place on the side altar at seven in the morning. To hell with them, thought a horrified Gunter, who was now determined that they would have a civic marriage. Una, however, was dead set on a church wedding, and so they were married quietly, on a side altar, one bright summer morning in May, following the ceremony with a simple wedding meal in Wicklow.

A condition of their parole was that Gunter and Goertz

had to report periodically to the Aliens Registration Office in Dublin Castle. On one such visit to the castle, both Gunter and Goertz were informed that the authorities were to take them that day to Mountjoy prison, with a view to deportation for questioning by the Allies. The two spies were in adjoining cells when they were given the news. Goertz was aghast. Gunter's war was definitely over but Goertz, increasingly demented, was still fighting in his head. He was devastated by Germany's defeat and couldn't contemplate surrender under any circumstances, especially because his home town was now under Soviet control. To be returned home to Allied interrogation would be to face the reality of this defeat.

In the holding cell, Gunter had just been joined by his new wife when they heard a thud from the cell next door. They looked around the corner and saw Goertz's two outstretched legs on the floor. He had taken his own life rather than face deportation. The guards rushed into Gunter's cell to try and prevent him doing the same, but he assured them that he had no intention of doing so. Goertz had had a cavity ring that he wore from the first day he landed in Ireland, within which was concealed a phial of cyanide. This personal escape route was on him for the seven years he'd been in Ireland, but the authorities never suspected it. With his imminent return to a defeated Germany now unavoidable, Goertz opened the ring, tossed his head back and died for his country at his own hand. He was buried in Dean's Grange cemetery in south Dublin, his coffin draped in a large swastika. His remains were subsequently re-interred in the German military cemetery in Glencree, County Wicklow.

BREAK-OUT!

Jan Van Loon, Gunter's partner in escape crime, joined two of his fellow spies in a successful joinery business in Dublin after the war. He managed to avoid deportation and still lives in north County Dublin. Gunter was duly returned to Frankfurt in a United States military aircraft, where he stayed in a luxurious *schloss* whilst being de-briefed. After a three-week interrogation, he was released without charge and made his way to Hamburg where his new Irish wife soon joined him. There he was reunited with his displaced family who, along with the other Germans in the eastern provinces, had been forced at gunpoint, by the German army, to make the journey westwards as the Russians advanced. The Schutzes were effectively ethnically cleansed out of Silesia. Gunter's work was to bring him over and back to Ireland and he ultimately settled there, dying in 1996 in Avoca, County Wicklow. Throughout the rest of his life, it can be assumed that he had no further occasion to don his famous feminine escape costume.

Come Hell or
High Water

AROUND THE SAME TIME AS THE BRITISH were executing their
great escapes from Nazi prisoner-of-war camps, twenty-one
IRA internees shimmied along an underground tunnel leading out of Derry prison. They had spent the previous six
months excavating the forty-five-foot tunnel, and had
broken through to the surface into a coalshed on the outside
only a week before. There was scarcely enough room in
some sections to crawl, and they had to shuffle along on
their bellies. As they inched their way forward, they knew
that every dark, cramped, dirty inch led them closer to that
dreamt-of state of freedom. Once outside the prison, it
would be a short five-mile journey to the border and the
security of the Free State. Suddenly, the shuffling forward
stopped. Word was passed down the line of men that the
mouth of the tunnel appeared to be filled in. Had the
authorities discovered it?

▲▲▲

When war had broken out in 1939, it was clear to the authorities in Northern Ireland that they would have to quell any

subversives or would-be insurrectionists. Internment was introduced and all known republican activists rounded up and sent to the Crumlin Road jail in Belfast, some of them as young as sixteen. They were arrested on the grounds that they 'were suspected of being about to act in a manner prejudicial to the maintenance of the peace in Northern Ireland. It is expedient that they be interned at His Majesty's pleasure.' When Belfast jail was bursting at the seams, the authorities decided to re-open Derry's crumbling prison. The cold stone edifice of the Bastille-like fortress greeted one of these internees, Belfast's Albert Price, and as the gates slammed shut behind him, a shiver ran down his spine. The gothic exterior opened to an interior that was just as unwelcoming. It was dark, dreary and damp. The only respite from the cold stone walls was a small barred window. They could see the outside world going about its business, oblivious to the fate of these prisoners interned without trial. As he gazed at the faraway hills, Price's thoughts turned to escaping as one way of fighting this injustice. When he got out, he would show them just *how* prejudicially he could act towards His Majesty's government!

As some of the windows even lacked glass, the prisoners had to move their beds so that the snow that fell into their cells did not dampen their bedclothes. There was no heating in the prison and as winter approached, the internees felt the sharp northerly wind blowing through them, gnawing at their impotence. Some internees simply went under and became psychotic, two of them losing their minds and believing that they were saints. Others resolved to combat the regime responsible for their mistreatment. Sean McArdle was the OC (officer in command) of the IRA within the prison, and he gathered the internees together to discuss different means of resistance. First on the agenda was an escape bid and plans were soon afoot to investigate weaknesses in the system, with all ground-floor cells being investigated for digging potential. The age-old passive-aggressive weapon of a hunger strike was mooted but ruled out as counter-productive. McArdle was acutely aware that severe censorship was imposed on the press during the war, and any effort to highlight their cause was unlikely to achieve any worthwhile exposure. Others suggested a prison mutiny, which McArdle was not in favour of for the same reason, but as support for it amongst the prisoners was overwhelming, he gave it his reluctant blessing. Although Easter was a traditional time of rebellion in the republican calendar, Christmas Day was set as the date for the riot. If Easter was a time for sacrifice, Christmas was a time of re-birth and renewal and the prison authorities would never anticipate what was coming. Besides, the warders would be expecting an easy day of it.

That Christmas morning, Mass was a hushed affair. Although the prisoners were stirring with excitement, they had to ensure that the authorities suspected nothing. As they made their way from the small chapel in the yard back to their cells, the time to revolt had arrived. All the warders were aggressively overpowered and locked into empty cells. Within minutes, the prison was under the control of the IRA and the prisoners danced with joy, a victory dance. Republican banners, and the makeshift tricolours they had so assiduously sewn together in the run up to the riot, were proudly displayed from the cell windows. For a while, the prison's ominous façade was bedecked in green, white and gold, a colourful beacon of liberty on a dark December day.

Passers-by on Bishop Street were greeted with yells of triumph from the internees inside, but alas these were the only people on the outside who were to hear of their insurgence. Wartime censorship meant that the revolt scarcely caused a ripple in the news. Their moment in the sun was short-lived, as the authorities could not tolerate such a treasonous act in a time of war. How *dare* they? This time, they had really asked for it. When efforts to re-establish control of the prison failed, the RUC, the B Specials and the British Army brought in the Derry fire brigade, with their power hoses, to re-impose order. The rebellion was swiftly and severely quashed. The IRA surrendered, knowing that the game was up, but that they had made their point.

The RUC had some points of their own to make, however. The prisoners were made run the gauntlet between RUC men, B Specials and the army, who used batons and the butts of rifles to exact retribution for embarrassing them. Paddy Adams (the uncle of the current Sinn Féin president, Gerry Adams) and Sean McArdle (the OC) were singled out for particularly harsh treatment. All the rebels were then thrown into their bitterly cold cells, and the hoses were turned on them. Bruised and battered, and frozen to the skin, they were each given an orange as their Christmas dinner that day. The IRA bombed the Hawkins Street fire station early in the new year as an act of retribution.

McArdle knew that the riot was a tactical mistake. They had made no impact on the outside world and would now be given little freedom within the prison. A spooky silence descended that Christmas night, as the prisoners lay licking their wounds, a beaten force. Even those sharing cells couldn't utter a word. Deep in the night, a low murmuring emerged from Paddy Adams's cell. This murmuring grew in volume until it became recognisable as an old rebel song. Before long, all the prisoners were singing at the tops of their voices, reflecting on what they had achieved. They had got up off their knees, if only for a couple of hours. The *esprit de corps* was stirred up by the passionate singing and one thing became clear that night: if anybody was going to get them out of this place, it was Paddy Adams, a true leader of men.

▲▲▲

Following this severe backlash, rioting was ruled out as a means of protest and the prisoners' attention turned towards an escape bid and an escape committee was formed. Already etched into Derry prison's republican folklore was how Frank Carty was sprung from the prison on the morning of his court-martial, on 21 February 1921. Carty, the story goes, was captured by the Black and Tans in Tubbercurry, County Sligo, and transferred north to the maximum-security prison in Derry. He had been accused of the murder of two RIC officers and the forthcoming court-martial was sure to hand down a death sentence. Sligo prison was deemed unsuitable for holding him as he had already been sprung from there the previous year. In its ninety-six years as a prison, nobody had ever escaped from Derry, but then it had never housed Frank Carty before. Nor was it ever pitted against that loveable rogue of a Derryman, Charles 'Nomad' McGuinness, who was later to offer aid to a certain Gunter Schutz!

McGuinness smuggled in a hacksaw blade, a length of fisherman's line and some black soap to Carty, who was to feign illness in order to be transferred to the hospital wing. There he was to cut the bars on the window, concealing the cut with black soap. McGuinness, on the outside, had assembled a rope ladder, which Carty was to haul up to his cell window using the fishing line. Tying this to the bars he would have a rope bridge to the perimeter wall, from where he could clamber down the wall into Harding Street and, with his partner in crime McGuinness, disappear into the night.

In the dead of night, with his court-martial only hours away, Carty heard McGuinness's signal and cast the weighted fishing line over the wall. He hauled up the ladder and tied it to the bars of his cell, creating an anchor for his bridge to freedom. He was a big lad, and only after much kicking and heaving did he manage to squeeze through the bars. He crawled gingerly along the rope-bridge, concentrating on McGuinness's silhouette on the opposite wall. Don't look down, he repeated to himself like a mantra, as forty feet beneath him was the darkest, most deathly part of the prison: its cemetery. One last heave and he made it to the outside wall, and then scrambled down to the back yard of one of the unionist-owned houses in Harding Street where McGuinness awaited him. Whilst scurrying down Abercorn Road, their ears were pricked for the sound of the cannon boom from the prison, signalling a break-out. Fleeing towards the Catholic ghettos, they scattered cayenne pepper in their wake to dispel the bloodhounds. The next day Carty was smuggled on to McGuinness's father's boat, the *Carricklea*, and set sail for Scotland, having proved that 'fortress Derry' was not impregnable.

What was clear from Carty's example was that outside help

would be required to effect an escape and, since after the riots the prisoners were not permitted any visits, letters or parcels, such endeavours temporarily went off the agenda. It wasn't until a few months later, after St Patrick's Day 1940, that they were allowed to receive visitors again and could therefore communicate with the outside world. Their escape plans, however, were cut short later that year, when Derry prison was deemed unfit for housing internees and, while it was being renovated, all the mutineers were transferred to the prison ship *Al Rawdah* until Derry was ready for their return. The government of Northern Ireland had acquired this disused frigate ship, which they moored in Strangford Lough, to house the swelling numbers of internees. Not unlike the British soldiers in Colditz, these republican internees were hell-bent on escaping, but the *Al Rawdah* proved a very effective holding centre. It was moored off Killyleagh in County Down, at a point where two tides met, making any attempt at swimming to freedom extremely hazardous, if not impossible.

As De Valera's government in the South had also introduced internment by this stage, nearly all active republicans were behind bars and the IRA leadership were now desperate to spring some of their volunteers from prison. IRA activity amounted to little more than several foiled attempts to burn down cinemas showing British newsreels. The organisation firmly believed in the old republican maxim of England's difficulty being Ireland's opportunity. After all, the insurrection of 1798 was made possible because the old enemy was fighting against Napoleon, the 1916 rising was made possible because the empire was fighting on another front and this opportunity, whilst England was again at war, needed to be exploited. No avenue was left unexplored by the IRA in getting some of their number off the prison ship and back into active service, and one south Down volunteer came up with a novel idea to realise this. A technical expert, he had invented a torpedo that could be launched across Strangford Lough, blowing a hole in the side of the *Al Rawdah* and turning it into a nice playground for the fishies. All the internees would be able to swim back into active service! The plan was sent to GHQ of the IRA but, not surprisingly, was ruled out as they feared that they could lose lives.

▲▲▲

One of those on the boat was Jimmy O'Hagan, from Kilkeel in south Down, who had been sent here from Belfast jail in the course of his own escape plan. Jimmy's parents owned a pub and greengrocers on the main street of the town, which was mixed between unionists and nationalists. When the Twelfth of July came each year, the pavements were bedecked with Union Jacks erected on barrels to greet the parade. Of course one of these flags would always be prominently positioned outside their shop. 'Go out there like a good lad and kick that barrel down the steps,' his mother would tell him and he would always oblige. It was no surprise, then, that in the middle of one night in 1939 the young Jimmy was picked up and interned in Belfast jail, and it was there that the internees got a taste for digging tunnels to freedom. They tunnelled from their cells to the prison yard, then under air-raid shelters towards the perimeter wall, and had only fifteen feet to go when they were transferred to the prison ship *Al Rawdah*. One advantage for the authorities of moving the prisoners from place to place was that it often thwarted escape attempts such as these.

The *Al Rawdah* may have been poorly designed for housing prisoners, but it was certainly escape-proof. O'Hagan, whilst exercising on deck, was able to look at the mainland where, without a breadwinner in the family, his wife and child were struggling to make ends meet. He noticed that a delivery boat pulled up alongside the *Al Rawdah* every week, and he and four comrades saw an opportunity to stow away on the boat as it left for dry land. As night fell, they loosened a panel from the side of the ship and this gave them access to the supply boat. They landed on the smaller boat with a thud, and proceeded to look for a suitable hiding place on deck. A young crew-man heard the thump as they landed, and came on deck to investigate. He saw the dark figures and screamed, 'The Germans, the Germans!' thinking that an invasion was underway. In the confusion, the internees tried to scramble back to their bunk beds on the main ship but one man, Joe McNabb, failed to get back in time and was caught in the act of escaping.

The only way off the prison ship, it seemed, was to die, and this fate befell one internee, Sean Gaffney. The OC on the ship, Neill Gillespie from Derry, delivered the oration which commenced: 'One of our number has been released, released with honour, released unconditionally into the hands of God who made him…' Despite countless attempts, nobody ever successfully escaped from fortress *Al Rawdah*.

▲ ▲ ▲

BREAK-OUT!

However, escape was definitely in the air in 1941 and escape lore circulated rapidly. Back in Belfast jail, one of the IRA's most legendary escapees, Gerry 'The Bird' Doherty, was plotting his break for freedom. For this escape bid he teamed up with Eddie Keenan of Belfast. From the topmost cell in D wing, he could see that the 'ordinaries' in the next wing finished exercising at 12.15pm and 4.15pm each day, while the internees were not required to leave their yard until 12.30pm and 4.30pm. That left a window of fifteen minutes in which an escape could be executed across the ordinaries' wing. Between the two yards there was a corrugated iron fence that had to be surmounted, but to Doherty this was only a minor obstacle. He noticed great nuts holding each section of iron together, so he bent a soup ladle from the kitchen into the shape of a spanner that he could loosen them with.

The two of them chose their day in May 1941, opening the bolt in the iron fence with ease. So far, so good. They had manufactured a rope ladder from sheets, on the end of which was attached a crook made of wood, which they cast over the wall. It caught first time, but as soon as Doherty put his weight on it, it came crashing down on the inside. The wooden hook wouldn't work. There was nothing for it but to abandon the escape and return to the yard. Word spread around the jail about the failed attempt and they were approached by three others, Phil McTaggart, Liam Burke and Billy Watson, who were also eager for liberation. Doherty wasn't going to be let down by a wooden crook this time. The following day he broke the legs off a collapsible mess table, which made a much sturdier hook.

The five decided to try again that Friday, but to attempt the escape in the afternoon period this time. That day they were approached by two others, Harry O'Rawe and Paddy Doyle, who wished to join them on the escape. Although they were welcomed, they were told that they would be last to scale the wall. The corrugated fencing was again opened and peeled back, and all seven made their way to the perimeter wall. As the fourth man reached the top of the wall, the warders spotted them and came running to prevent the escape. Doherty himself, fifth to go over the wall, was scaling it when the warders reached him. They tried to haul him back down but were prevented from doing so by the two remaining prisoners, O'Rawe and Doyle, who were captured on the inside. As the Bird scampered over the wall, he was relieved that he had permitted the last two to come on the escape. The warders ransacked his cell only to discover he had etched the words: 'This Bird has flown' on the cell wall.

Once out, Watson, Keenan and Burke leapt over another wall into a convent, where a fifteen-year-old novice, from County Clare, was praying peacefully. The three men landed in front of her, explaining that they had escaped from jail, that they were members of the IRA and that she would come to no harm. There was a moment's pause whilst she digested what they were saying, then she started to scream blue murder. Her mouth was covered by one of the men until the Mother Superior arrived. She simply said, 'Follow me, boys.' Triumph! The nearest Keenan had come to this exhilarating sensation was when, as a child, he used to sneak into the movies without paying. The Mother Superior led them through the convent and out the front door where, as luck would have it, the Burke's family doctor, a Dublin republican named Dr Harrington, was passing in his car. They escaped to the safety of the Lower Falls.

The fourth over the wall, McTaggart, was an Ardoyne man who knew the area and easily made his way to safety. Doherty, the last over, made his way through a nearby school and out on to the street. As he passed a row of terraced houses, he saw a votive light in one of the windows and entered, knowing it to be a Catholic home. An old lady lived there and he asked her if she knew anybody in the movement. She called up to a young man tiling her roof, who was a volunteer, and Doherty was whisked to a safe house. This Bird had indeed flown.

Not all escapes were so successful, however. Kevin Kelly, later transferred to Derry prison, was busy plotting an escape from the second floor of Belfast jail's D wing. He had smuggled hacksaw blades in the seam of an attaché case, and managed to saw through the window bars. He installed a dummy in his bed and, together with Seamus Twomey (who was later to escape from Mountjoy by helicopter in 1973), made a bid for freedom on a cold March evening. They had made a rope ladder from bedsheets, with which Kelly lowered himself out the window. The intention was to drape blankets over the barbed wire that hung between the cell wall and an outer wall, and dash across. The wire would not hold him, however. While he was trying to negotiate it, a warder spotted him and raised the alarm, at which point Kelly scampered back up the rope. A headcount was ordered immediately and the warders discovered that there seemed to be one prisoner too many. They had counted the dummy! Kelly, Twomey and another prisoner called Russell were not charged with attempting to escape, but they were brought before a magistrate in the jail and sentenced to twenty-one days' bread and water for the destruction of Crown property.

▲▲▲

The internees in Belfast jail were constantly on the lookout for new escape routes, as the jail had holes appearing in it all the time. It would not be so in Derry prison, which was re-opened in 1942 and received prisoners from Belfast and return prisoners from the *Al Rawdah*. Among them were Paddy Adams and Jimmy O'Hagan. Governor Fryer watched from his garden in the prison as the seven buses arrived containing the handcuffed internees. He turned to his wife and said, 'I'm afraid, my dear, this means trouble.' One of those internees, Niall Gillespie from Derry, remembered having approached the governor three years before, after the riots of 1939, to ask for medical help for those who were injured. 'If these men are not dead or their throats cut, I can do nothing for them, Gillespie,' came the reply. As further batches of internees landed in the prison, they decided on a new command structure with Paddy Adams as OC and Jimmy O'Hagan as adjutant. Adams was still licking his wounds from the riot and he was determined to assert himself against the governor in subtler, less confrontational ways.

Under the leadership of Adams and O'Hagan, the internees began to organise themselves along quasi-military lines. Prisoners had to be addressed by the prison officers through the OC on each floor, who in turn reported to Adams. The IRA's first battle of wills against the governor was a minor one, but showed nonetheless what could be achieved through organised resistance. The internees demanded the right to prepare and cook their own food, and negotiated with Governor Fryer that all non-internees should be removed from the kitchens. When this was refused, the internees started a hunger strike in which they refused to eat food they had not prepared themselves. In many respects, Fryer simply wanted an easy life and soon granted the prisoners' wishes. The governor, who had fought in the Russian civil war against the Bolsheviks, would often say to the internees, 'I had five thousand White Russians under me and they didn't give me as much trouble as you fellows!'

An escape committee was established, and it was decreed that any escape bids had to come through this central committee for approval. A number of prisoners came up with the idea of tunnelling under the cell where one of the internees, Billy Graham, was housed, and digging towards the back of the prison to Harding Street. After some initial trials, this plan seemed to have potential and was adopted by the IRA camp staff.

The first attempted escape pre-empted this plan, however, and was undertaken by a young detainee called Catherwood. As he wasn't a republican, he feared he would not receive the approval of the committee so he determined to make his own bid for liberty. He figured that the least-guarded side of the prison was where Governor Fryer's residence was, and he and two accomplices proceeded to tunnel into the governor's garden, from where they would scale the perimeter wall.

Fryer and his wife were sitting in their private garden, enjoying the late-afternoon sun, when they noticed a figure emerging from the grass. Was this a mole? As Catherwood and his accomplices emerged through the surface, Fryer had by this time assembled a number of officers to escort the escapees back to their cells. It was not a particularly well-thought-through escape plan, and it was foolish to attempt it during the day. When news of this foiled attempt reached the IRA command structure they were furious, and Catherwood was on the sticky end of a severe reprimanding. Adams told him that all escapes had to be centrally approved, but what he didn't tell him was that he could have jeopardised the IRA's own escape bid, which had already been started from underneath Billy Graham's cell.

In October 1942, when the tunnelling commenced, it was essential that only a small clique knew about it. Loose talk or bravado could jeopardise the operation. The internees had free association during the day, but were able to make excuses and return to their cells, should they so wish. The newly laid wooden floors of Graham's cell were removed and a volunteer started the painstaking digging, descending deeper and deeper. Sean McGreevey, who shared the cell with Graham, was a deeply religious man and would bless each tunneller with holy water as he descended into the shaft. As clothes were scarce and frequent dirt on them was sure to be noticed by the guards, the diggers would be stripped naked except for a pullover worn unconventionally, tied around the waist with their legs through the sleeves. The pullovers never left the cell. Most of the tunnelling was done during the day as the internees' free association meant that they would not be missed, but as time progressed and impatience increased, those in Graham's cell started to dig by night. Two of the men would dig while another would keep watch for the warder, who would shine his torch on each bed to satisfy himself that nobody had gone AWOL. By the time the warder reached the cell, the diggers had been given a signal, and had scrambled up the shaft and leapt into bed, feigning a deep sleep.

The digging was quiet enough, but the sound of the floorboards being lifted made quite a racket. In order to smother the sound during the day, deafening *uillinn* pipe lessons were organised by Billy Murray in the Nissen hut closest to the escape cell. As the diligent students caterwauled on their chanters, the diggers sank a sixteen-foot shaft into the ground using the outer wall of the prison as a support. There was a gap of two feet between the floorboards of Graham's cell and the ground below, and most of the clay and stones were stashed here at first.

As the tunnel progressed, though, the clay had to be moved elsewhere and the internees were organised like worker ants. Tom McArdle discovered that, underneath the boards in his cell, there were steps into a four-foot-deep cellar. Most of the larger rocks that had been removed were stored here. The rest of the clay was moved stealthily by the prisoners. Some secreted it under their oxters, concealed by a jacket that was casually slung over the shoulder. Others were able to fold the clay into their shirts, which they looped and tucked into their trousers. It was a short trip to the lavatory in the middle of the exercise yard, where the clay could be surreptitiously dispersed around the yard itself or dumped down the toilet. During the six months of the tunnelling the plumbing had to be fixed twice by the unsuspecting authorities, who blamed the clogging on the antiquated infrastructure in the ancient prison.

Every conceivable implement was used for the dig, including forks, spoons, and the legs from trestle tables; even the handle of a bucket proved very effective. The boys from the *Al Rawdah* had managed to bring marlinspikes, which were used traditionally to mend fishing nets, into the prison. These were ten-inch tapered spikes that inmates often used to make rings from coins. Once a hole was made in a coin, the marlinspike could be hammered through the coin until it was shaped like a ring. These spikes took on another function in Derry, however; they were the most effective implements for digging. Once the excavation had reached the bottom of the prison foundations, the tunnelling changed direction, heading at a gradually ascending angle towards the perimeter wall. At this depth the diggers needed a light by which to work. The boys who worked in the kitchen made very effective candles from stored-up cooking fat, through which a strip of sheet was pulled as a wick. Tin lids made ideal candleholders. In addition to shedding light on proceedings, the candles could also be used to monitor the amount of oxygen remaining in the tunnel. If the candle guttered out, it was time to call a halt as they risked fainting and suffocating.

Going sideways was slower and more difficult than going straight down. As each few yards were cleared, the ceiling had to be propped up to avoid a collapse. Sandbags made from pillowcases and filled with stones lined both sides of the tunnel, holding the earth aloft. Pieces of wood and old furniture, groaning under its weight, were commandeered to prop up the sixteen feet of dense clay, which could collapse and suffocate them in an instant. Progress was slowed further when the tunnel reached an underground rivulet. Painstakingly, as if on a sinking ship, the excavators worked at bailing out the water, but with each passing day the tunnel was filling with more and more water, and erosion was proving a problem too. It needed to be shored up. A few weeks of strategic damming reinforced and strengthened this damp patch, but the tunnellers always hastened through this particular section as it was never very stable.

One day, a volunteer had managed to shimmy swiftly past this section, and was making progress on extending the tunnel into the endless blackness, when something glistening caught his attention. He brought his makeshift candle closer to inspect it. Buried treasure? He cleared the soil from around the shiny object, and a golden handle was uncovered. It was a coffin! Terrified, he scrambled back up the tunnel to the cell and told his comrades. Most of the internees at this time were God-fearing, Mass-going Catholics and this discovery gave them the heebie-jeebies. Those less superstitious were sent to work on this section, and diverted the passage underneath the coffin. One consolation was that the roof of the tunnel would be well supported at this point!

Above ground, the internees had settled into a life of prison routine. The food, though cooked by themselves, was the same old fare on any given day, week in and week out. The exception was one of those special occasions when a parcel was sent in from outside, and a feast would be prepared. One such time was Christmas 1942, when Chuck Sharkey opened his parcel to discover a mouth-watering roast ready to be devoured. He held it aloft and examined it – he had never seen anything quite like it before and indeed was suspicious of it. As he had grown up in the city, he was not accustomed to these farmyard animals. Quietly he showed it to another of the kitchen staff: 'Did you ever hear of a four-legged chicken?' he asked. 'That's a rabbit,' came the terse reply.

The best parcels were received by the three McKeown brothers from Lurgan, who seemed to get a substantial delivery every month, without fail. That Christmas, Governor Fryer summoned Pierce McKeown to his office, as a mouth-watering Christmas hamper had arrived for him. He greeted McKeown with the hamper laid out on his desk. Taking a bottle of whiskey from the parcel, Fryer said, 'I'm afraid this is going to hurt me as much as it is going to hurt you,' and, in front of Pierce's disbelieving eyes and salivating tongue, proceeded to pour the contents down the sink. The prisoners were not to be deterred by this, of course, and for the Christmas concert they made their own *poitín* in the exercise yard washhouse. As they celebrated, they pretended to themselves that the *poitín* almost tasted palatable. McKeown could only think of what he could have been drinking had it not been for Fryer. On Christmas night, Paddy Adams, Rocky Burns and Albert Price, the mutineers of 1939, reminisced about that night four years previously when the prison became a place of dread and they lay there vanquished, their hopes in tatters. As all three were in on the escape bid they looked forward to next Christmas, which they would enjoy on the far side of the wall.

▲▲▲

BREAK-OUT!

As Christmas gave way to the new year of 1943, it was clear that internment on both sides of the border was taking its toll on the IRA. This window of Ireland's opportunity was passing without a flutter. They simply did not have enough free personnel to mount any operations, and the only means of recruitment was to spring some of the IRA internees from jail. In Belfast, yet another daring escape plan was being put in place in Crumlin Road jail where the IRA Chief of Staff, Hugh McAteer, was serving a fifteen-year sentence for treason. Two other internees, Jimmy Steele and Pat Donnelly, had discovered an escape route that took them over the roof of the jail and, as he was vital to the organisation outside, they also brought McAteer in on it. As the plan was developing, they brought in Ned Maguire because he was an experienced slater by trade. Early on the morning of 15 January, the four prisoners received permission to go to the bathroom separately. There they leapt onto a table which was subsequently removed by other prisoners, made their way through a trapdoor in the roof and, with the expertise of Maguire at hand, were able to break through the roof tiles from within and descend into the yard below. The previous week they had manufactured a rope from bedsheets, with a crook they made from a brass bed-end bandaged to one end of it, which they were to hang from the barbed wire on top of the perimeter wall. Maguire stood on McAteer's shoulders and used a pole to attach the crook to the barbed wire. The first tug on the rope showed great resilience, and the four clambered over the wall. Despite being in prison uniform, they mingled with the early-morning workers going down the Crumlin Road on their way to the dockyards. The boys were back in town.

With a reward for £3,000 on his head, McAteer was rein-stated as Chief of Staff of the IRA and news reached him of the planned break-out of Derry prison. He called an IRA army conference to be held in the Short Strand area of the city, where they discussed the paucity of personnel operating on the ground. McAteer trusted those involved in the Derry escape and GHQ resolved to put its full support behind the escape bid.

Two plucky girls were supplying the staff on the outside with bulletins about the tunnel's progress. Paddy Adams's fiancée, Annie Hamill (whose brother Sean was also in on the Derry escape) was receiving letters from Adams written in code. Because all communication in and out of the prison was subject to scrutiny by the warders, Adams would dip his pen in milk and write secret messages between the lines of his letters. Annie heated the letters by the fire, the secret messages would appear like magic, and she would then pass these on to GHQ. Jimmy O'Hagan's sister, Mary Theresa, lived in Letterkenny, County Donegal, and was able to visit Derry frequently, where she would also receive communications and, indeed, point the tunnelling in the right direction, towards Harding Street (not far from where Frank Carty had escaped twenty-two years previously).

The excavators were sure they were moving in the right direction, but they needed to know what distance they had travelled, and at what point they would surface. To measure this they required a catapult and searched around for the best material, but initial experiments with the elastic from an old pair of underpants were none too effective. One of the volunteers had a better idea. Much to the chagrin of the foot-ballers, a leather football was commandeered and the rubber bladder inside cut up to make a considerably better sling-shot. With some thread attached to a lead weight, they could fire the weight over the perimeter wall and measure the distance required for the tunnel. Necessity, after all, is the mother of invention. From the second-floor window, under cover of darkness, a volunteer pulled the slingshot with all his strength and let the weight fly. It fell hopelessly short. On the second attempt, he left some slack thread outside the window and fired again, this time making the distance to the perimeter wall. He then reeled in the weight until he saw it fall into the prison, then marked that point on the thread. This thread was then used to measure the distance required for the tunnel. It was an exact science.

There was not a lot left on the coil of thread, thought Billy Graham as he dug diligently forward, advancing the tunnel slowly but surely. As he dug, Eddie Steele moved the exca-vated clay towards the mouth of the tunnel, just underneath their cell. This was a routine they did, day in and day out, and at this stage he was just going through the motions. As he returned to the end of the tunnel, disaster struck. The damp patch of the tunnel had caved in and Graham was trapped behind it, encased in a clay coffin. He had turned when he heard the collapse but there was no way through. He frantically burrowed his way back through the debris. He began to panic as he noticed his candle had extin-guished through lack of oxygen, and he felt himself weaken. Frantically his comrades tore at the freshly fallen rubble until finally they could hear him – he was still conscious. His relieved comrades pulled him through to safety.

Although aware that they had narrowly avoided tragedy, they were unbowed by this, simply reinforcing that section of the tunnel and proceeding apace. As the thread told them that they neared the perimeter wall, they decided to tunnel at an angle that would bring them closer to the surface. Nearing the surface, they noticed a large rock blocking the way. Further excavation revealed this to be the perimeter wall: its foundations were as deep as the prison's walls, so they had to backtrack nearly twenty feet into the tunnel and proceed straight ahead rather than upwards. Though this Y in the tunnel set their timing back somewhat, it proved useful as this redundant passageway was now used to store surplus debris from further digging. The long journey back through the tunnel to the cell was no longer necessary.

As the day of the escape approached, it was decided that twenty people should come, and once those twenty had made it through the tunnel, it was then open to anybody else who could make it. A free-for-all. Senior members of the IRA were approached to come on the escape, but a strict precondition was laid down that any escapee would have to be ready and willing to return to the armed struggle. However, the army on the outside was reeling from a scandal. The Chief of Staff, Stephen Hayes, had been captured, held hostage and allegedly tortured into a confession of his spying activity for the Free State government. As a result of this, many republicans were reluctant to return to an organisation that either had allowed a traitor to be promoted to its highest office, or wrongfully forced a confession from an innocent man. Whatever side of the Hayes affair one was on, it gave reason to mistrust this organisation that appeared to be in tatters, and some declined to join in on the escape. Many more were gung-ho, however, and the twenty were selected, with word going out through Paddy Adams's letters to Annie that the tunnel was nearing its final phase.

▲▲▲

The IRA on the outside knew that two things were required to make the escape a success: money and arms. An arms raid on the RAF barracks on Belfast's Newtownards Road was sanctioned to obtain guns and ammunition for the escapees. Louis Duffin was in charge of the raid, but his entrance into the barracks was discovered immediately. As the alarm was raised Duffin legged it to the getaway car, which was at this stage driving off, being pursued by an RUC police car. Duffin failed to board the car and collapsed in the street, clutching his gun in his pocket, and thinking his number was up. The RUC car stopped. Duffin was picked up by the RUC man, who dusted him off and said, 'They nearly killed you, son.' He was conveyed to the nearest tram station in the police car, the RUC man all the while bemoaning the lawlessness of Belfast's drivers. A raid was also sanctioned on a horse-drawn van in Strabane, County Tyrone. The OC of Tyrone, and his adjutant, were to carry out the Dick Turpin-esque hold-up. In the early-morning darkness on 2 February, the Royal Mail van driver and his helper rode out of their depot in the train station with a cargo of letters for the province. Frost glistened on the empty streets. As they left the station, a dark figure approached them, shining a light in their eyes. The figure grabbed hold of the horse's reins and ordered the driver to dismount at gunpoint. As he did so, another figure sprang into the carriage with a light, where he segregated registered packages from ordinary mail. With the substantial amount of £1,500, the two made off on bicycles.

Back inside the prison, as the tunnel neared completion, Adams and O'Hagan were looking for signs that the escape bid had leaked to the authorities. They knew that the plot had been kept as secret as possible, but they were worried that it was almost going *too* smoothly. If the authorities knew about it, were they just toying with them, letting them toil and labour only to foil the escape as the tunnel neared completion? Underground, the diggers could hear the sounds of dogs barking and they knew that the outside world beckoned. It was not far now. As they inched their way to the surface, Billy Graham was elected to be the first to poke his head through. In the back of their minds was the discomfiting thought that the RUC or the army could simply be waiting for them as they popped out of the hole, picking them off one by one in the act of escaping. Jimmy O'Hagan was so worried that this fate awaited them he asked his brother not to go on the escape so that he could look after O'Hagan's wife and child in the event that the escapees were slain.

Graham wasn't completely sure that they were on the right side of the perimeter wall. He paused a moment, took a deep breath and stuck his head through to the surface. Cold, fresh air was sucked into the tunnel, and Graham breathed it in with delight as he looked at his surroundings. There was no prison yard, and there were no armed soldiers. He brought a candle through the hole, and looked at the four walls of a coal shed belonging to one of the houses on Harding Street. As he swung the candle around, he saw a brand-new shovel leaning against the wall as if mocking him, and he thought of the last six months of painful toil and digging, often with his bare hands. He could only laugh! Later that night, with considerable glee, Paddy Adams dipped his pen in milk and sent word to the outside that zero hour was to be 8.30am on Saturday, 21 March. After a grand total of fifteen tons of clay had been dispersed around the prison, the forty-five-foot shaft was finally complete.

On Friday, 20 March, Jimmy Steele and Liam Burke hired a furniture van, with a driver, from Curran Bros. of Belfast. This was to be the getaway vehicle for the escape. On the journey from Belfast, the driver stopped at an RUC station to deliver a message. 'What message?' Steele asked him, trying not to sound too alarmed. It seemed innocent enough. It was too early to commandeer the vehicle, so Steele had to sit tight in the cab while the driver went into the barracks. For all he knew, the driver could be giving the game away inside. Time ticked on. What's keeping him? Steele thought. As he sat there, his eyes drifted to a noticeboard outside the barracks, and he realised that he recognised a face on one of the posters. He ought to, for it was his own. The reward poster read: '£3,000 will be paid to the person or persons furnishing information to the police leading to the arrest of any of the persons whose photographs and descriptions are given hereunder, and who escaped from Belfast prison on the morning of 15 January 1943.' His description stated that he had a sharp pointed chin and a slight build, a description he thought wasn't very flattering. The driver, obviously unaware of his passenger's dubious fame, emerged from the barracks and, to Steele's relief, simply hopped back in and proceeded to Derry.

On arrival in Derry, Steele produced a revolver and informed the driver that the van was being commandeered by the IRA. After he had explained what they were about, the driver told Steele that the revolver wouldn't be necessary, as he was a sympathiser. Indeed, a sense of adventure overtook him and he asked to be included in the escape bid. He explained that he could drive the van better than anybody else could, and he would be their best bet as a getaway driver. They agreed on this and were all billeted in a house in the city, while the furniture van was parked in Abercorn Place, adjacent to Harding Street. That night Steele reinforced the inside of the van in an attempt to make it bulletproof, and they settled down for a sleepless night.

The Logue family, who lived in 15 Harding Street, also had a sleepless night. Mrs Logue, a nervous sleeper at the best of times, was convinced that she could hear voices and rustling in the back yard, which their bedroom window overlooked. She peered out a number of times but could see nothing untoward. Her husband, now awake, suggested that it was probably just cats on the prowl.

On the other side of the great wall of Derry's prison, another twenty men woke from a night of disturbed sleep. 'Good morning,' a warder called McGregor said to Kevin Kelly, the would-be escapee, on his way to breakfast. 'It is a good morning, but I think there's going to be changes,' Kelly replied, but McGregor didn't notice the spring in his step. None of the escapees bothered to eat their breakfast as adrenalin was feeding their appetites. The regime in Derry was more relaxed than that in Belfast, and it didn't take much of an excuse to return to one's cell during the day; a lie-down or a read was sufficient reason. The escape was brilliantly stage-managed. They were well drilled: 'Remember, you are not escaping from a fire, you're just going about your normal prison business.' The chosen twenty made their way to Billy Graham's cell in a calm and orderly manner. Old Billy Murray was instructed to belt out a rousing reel on his *uillinn* pipes to cover the noise of the escape activity, but the boys were already dancing a jig with expectation.

Silently, the escapees shimmied down the muddy passage, but as those in front approached the mouth of the tunnel, they noticed to their dismay that the expected gust of air was no longer there. It's been filled in, thought the men in the vanguard, the tunnel has been discovered. Word passed from man to man back down the line, and their dejection was tangible. Adams pulled at the surface and discovered to his relief that it was coal. The Logues had ordered two bags of coal the day before, which had been thrown in on top of the tunnel entrance. A palpable sense of relief swept back through the men crammed into the damp, dark passage. All the coal had to be dragged back through the tunnel and stashed in the moribund section of the Y. Meanwhile, some of the escapees, who had not been in the tunnel before, began to panic in the darkness and the eighth man passed out. Albert Price, who had chosen to be ninth as this was his lucky number, cursed his luck at this point. As he pushed the dark figure in front of him, the seventh man pulled the unconscious heap by the hair.

They assembled as many men as possible in the coal shed before they moved out. Paddy Adams grabbed hold of the shovel, smashed the lock on the door and burst through into the yard, blinded by the morning light after spending so long in the darkness. As he made his way across the Logues' yard to their back door, he joyfully inhaled the fresh air, which tasted as sweet as honey, the very stuff of freedom.

After a disturbed night's sleep, Mr Logue woke in an irascible state that Saturday morning. He was dressing in the front parlour whilst his daughter Mollie, in her nightdress, prepared the breakfast in the back kitchen. As the rashers sizzled in the pan, she thought she saw a man in the backyard. Another quickly followed, and she was astounded to see a whole swarm of men emerging from the coal shed. She was astonished that such a small shed could hold so many people. As the filthy men came through the kitchen, one of them, Sean Hamill, moved her to one side and explained to her that everything was going to be all right, that they were just passing through and she would not be harmed if she kept quiet. As he left her, he noticed a fingerprint in coal dust on her back. A devout Catholic, Hamill felt a deep shame at touching a girl's naked skin. He had tarnished her. Mr Logue, hearing the commotion in the kitchen, hurriedly tried to pull on his trousers and investigate. He had managed to get his long johns on, but was struggling to get his second leg through his trousers when the train of men passed by the door. He stood there in disbelief, with one leg in and one out of his trousers. Still in her nightdress, Mrs Logue came down to find out what the fuss was all about, but stopped on the stairs when she saw what was going on. One of the men told her to be careful or she would catch cold. In all it was a calm affair, with the unsolicited guests passing through without incident.

BREAK-OUT!

Once the initial twenty had shimmied through, the tunnel was open to all, and word quickly passed among the other internees about what was going on. The warders' suspicions were aroused because a crowd of prisoners was milling around the door at the end of the wing. Warders thought a fight had broken out in Billy Graham's cell and went to investigate. By this stage, only one 'unofficial' escapee had managed to get through the tunnel; it was Jimmy O'Rawe, whose brother, Harry, one of the chosen few, had ensured that he was on standby as number twenty-one. Jimmy, a big man, got stuck in a narrow section of the tunnel, and ended up a good deal delayed behind the others. The other unofficial escapees were unaccustomed to the tunnel and many turned back, thinking that the other end of their road to freedom had been discovered. At the inside mouth of the tunnel, the warders had regained control, the alarm was raised and the RUC and B Specials were called into the prison.

Paddy Adams opened the front door of 15 Harding Street to be greeted by Liam Burke. They shook hands, and then Burke handed him a revolver. Coming just behind him, Kevin Kelly was also handed a gun, then pointed in the direction of the flight of steps down Abercorn Terrace, past the front door of the home of an RUC man, to the waiting furniture van. As he ran the fifty yards, Kelly felt he was walking on air. One spring from the bottom of the steps carried him into the back of the van, but not before he whacked his shin off it. It concerned him little. Burke waited at the front door for a little longer, but he left his post when it appeared that no more men were coming. Afraid that the other end of the tunnel had been discovered, he ran down the flight of steps and told the van driver to get moving. With the thrill-seeking driver at the helm, they sped in the direction of the Derry/Donegal border, and the escapees yelled in triumph when the van crossed the border at Carrigans. They were in the Free State. Surely De Valera, an ex-IRA man himself, would empathise with this daring escape and grant them their freedom?

De Valera had famously escaped from Lincoln jail on 3 January 1919, when he had been working as an altar server in the chapel. The prison chaplain had carelessly left a security key on the altar and De Valera, using a large candle, was able to take an impression of the key by pressing it into the hot wax. A duplicate key was then smuggled into the prison in a birthday cake. It was Michael Collins who orchestrated his safe passage to secure houses and back to the independence struggle. Although, given De Valera's own escape, the Derry men hoped he would welcome them, they suspected deep down that he couldn't be trusted. The southern government had hanged more IRA men during the course of World War II than the Stormont government had.

The escapees sped to an agreed rendezvous outside St Johnston, near Letterkenny, and were bundled into a shed. An IRA volunteer then drove the van back across the border to Sion Mills and tied up the van driver, faking a hijacking. The hire fee of nine pounds was forwarded to Curran Bros., much to their bemusement.

The B Specials and the RUC were called in to the prison to restore order amongst the giddy inmates, who were now singing and celebrating. They were ordered back to their cells for a headcount, but like mischievous goats on a mountainside, if they saw a gap to the left or right, they darted through it or entered the wrong cells in order to spread confusion. The cells for three people were found to contain only two, and the single cells appeared to be completely empty, or so it seemed until one looked behind the door. The warders got their vengeance, though. There was no physical violence but the cells were ransacked for handicraft materials and books, pens were taken away and all musical instruments were confiscated. Old Billy Murray's *uillinn* pipes were singled out for special attention, as much for their infernal din as for their role in the escape. Visits and parcels were suspended indefinitely and the hard-won concession of cooking their own food was lost. The kitchen was soon populated again by ordinaries.

▲▲▲

The next batch of men, Harry O'Rawe, Hubert McInerney, Brendan O'Boyle, Chips McCusker and the key figure of the dig, Billy Graham, emerged through the front door of the Logues' house only to discover that they had missed their ride. Their escort had disappeared, and the van was nowhere to be seen. Billy Graham was particularly dismayed, as he had stayed behind to help others through the tunnel he knew so well, only to be left behind. They made their way to the city cemetery, where they laid low until nightfall, then set off on foot, heading cross-country until they reached Letterkenny. Utterly exhausted, they made contact with a priest who brought them to his house, cleaned them up and brought all five of them out for a lip-smacking four-course meal. They couldn't believe their luck, especially when, the following day, they read of the fate of their comrades.

The main body of escapees, fourteen in all, had been given arms in the shed in St Johnston. They were each issued a rifle or a revolver, and they had a machine-gun in their possession also. The Northern Ireland authorities alerted the Gardaí and the Free State army. A huge manhunt was mounted in Donegal under Superintendant Tom Kelly, and the Killybegs D Company and Finner Camp's B Company were mobilised to scour the country around St Johnston. Jimmy McMonagle, the commanding officer in Letterkenny barracks, armed his team to track down the fugitives. The escapees watched from behind an elevated ditch on Kinacally mountain as the Free State soldiers formed a cordon and approached. All their preparation and hard work, all six months of it, were in vain, as they were sure to be caught. They were badly let down by the outside help.

Paddy Kelly, one of the IRA men on the outside facilitating the escape, was in possession of £700 for the escapees, which he manage to slip to a local farmer for the IRA to retrieve later. Some of the escapees were ready to blast their way out of this predicament, but orders came from the OC to dump their weapons into the ditch. No Free State soldiers were to be harmed in this operation. The main body of the escapees gave themselves up in order that a few of them, who had managed to slip away with a group of locals, could make good their getaway. These four, Jimmy Trainor, Alfie White, Rocky Burns, and Jimmy McGreevey, all managed to evade capture on the hillside. As the main body emerged from the field towards the army they were sure of lenient treatment from the Saorstát, which showed how naive they were of conditions in the South. The nervous and inexperienced Free State soldiers, often prodding them in the back with their rifles, escorted them down the mountain at gunpoint. From there they were brought to Letterkenny police barracks, where they all shared one cell, and a prison officer from Derry was brought in to identify them. However, they were assured that they would not be handed back to the Northern authorities. The escapees celebrated that night, singing an old favourite deep into the night:

> 'Oro my brown haired maiden
> I'll meet you in the glen ...'

The next day, they thought they were free men when, emblazoned across the front pages of the newspapers, was the headline, 'Éire Will Not Hand Back Internees.' They were then moved to Rock Hill barracks, which was a military post in Letterkenny, where they were kept in an underground cell until the following Friday. It was here that the escapees got their first taste of butter since the outbreak of war, and they relished it.

Having been wined and dined by the clergyman, the five late escapees were driven to a prominent IRA man in Ballybofey, Jimmy Clarke. It was decided that the five should make their way back to Dublin and make contact with GHQ to ascertain what their new roles would be. Brendan O'Boyle refused to go with them and decided to make his own way back to Belfast. He was never recaptured, but was later to die in violent circumstances. Clarke dressed the other four as cattle drovers, gave them each a blackthorn stick, and put them on a train from Sligo to Dublin. This was a grievous error as they were all from Belfast and lacked the contacts necessary to move secretly around the capital. On arrival there penniless, they made their way to the infamous republican B&B *An Stad*, where a welcoming committee of Branchmen greeted them and introduced them to the delights of internment, southern style. Handcuffed, they were ferried to the Curragh to sit out the remainder of the war.

Three of the four men who slipped away with the locals on the hillside were soon recaptured. The fourth, Alfie White, returned to Belfast to resume the struggle. Five weeks after the escape he was arrested at a safe house in the loyalist Windsor Drive and was sentenced to twelve years as a weapons dump was found in the house. Because of the way he'd had to move through the tunnel he was nicknamed 'Shuffles', and it stuck with him for the rest of his life.

As he had been on the run there before he was lifted, Sean Hamill knew Derry quite well, and after he came through the Logues' house he elected to make his own way through the city instead of boarding the van. He first sought refuge in a church, as by this stage the city was crawling with police, until nightfall. Then, when the wartime curfew left the streets empty, he made his way to a safe house he had stayed in whilst on the run. The residents couldn't believe their eyes when they saw who it was at the door. He was fêted as the great escapee, but nothing could stop every neighbour and relative dropping in to set eyes on the burrower. This was no longer secure. He was thinking whether or not to leave the house when another visitor came in, not to marvel at him but to bring him to safety.

BREAK-OUT!

Republican folklore has it that this new visitor was a chauffeur for one of the top unionists in Derry, and his car was probably the most secure hiding place in the city. They passed without fuss through the cordons and he was brought to a wealthy country area on the outskirts of the city, where he was hidden overnight. His chauffeur had a brainwave. Rather than trying to make it to the border on foot, he could join the Sunday hunt the next day. He was decked out in resplendent hunt regalia and helped on to a horse for the first time. The tunnel was a walk in the park compared to this, he thought to himself as bugles wailed, beagles howled, and the fox was set free with the huntsmen galloping in hot pursuit. Hamill didn't open his mouth for fear his accent would betray him, and lagged behind the enthusiastic hunt until he was able to detour towards the Donegal border. He felt a twinge of sympathy for the fox – the hunter, hunted.

The unofficial escapee, Jimmy O'Rawe, was the twenty-first and the last to emerge through the front door of the Logues' house. Harding Street was completely empty and he resolved to put as much distance as possible between himself and the prison. He lay low, sleeping rough in the city until Sunday evening when he decided to make his way on foot to the border. During the war, Derry was in darkness so movement around the city was reasonably easy. With the curfew in place, though, he knew if he was spotted at all, he would be lifted. As he made his way to the Letterkenny road, he was noticed by the RUC and gave himself up after a short pursuit.

On Friday, 27 March, the main body of internees were handcuffed in Rock Hill barracks and taken under armed escort in the direction of Dublin, stopping at Longford police barracks for a bland meal of raw fish and rock-hard peas. On arrival in the Curragh, the Derry escapees were asked which camp they wished to join. Brendan Behan once famously stated that the first item on the Irish political agenda was the split and, true to form, the Curragh was split down the middle between Liam Leddy's and Pierce Kelly's factions – a sure sign of a beaten organisation. Ignorant of the split, the escapees joined Kelly's gang simply because they recognised some fellow northerners on this side. Leddy issued the Derry escapees with an ultimatum: join our faction or be ostracised. Kevin Kelly went to the authorities and asked for a third kitchen to be opened for the Derry escapees, but his request was declined. Ostracism it would have to be, then.

Given refuge by a high-ranking member of the Free State army in Donegal, Sean Hamill gradually made his way unde-tected to Dublin, where he rejoined the ranks of the IRA. He teamed up with Frank Kerrigan, who had escaped from Mountjoy the previous October, and they swapped escape stories. In Mountjoy, Kerrigan and five other IRA men were given a small private room off the circle, ostensibly to learn Irish. They used a large timber log to smash the bars on the window sufficiently to squeeze through. Once on the out-side, they waited for the armed sentries to come down from the elevated posts they occupied at night, then they skedad-dled up the sentry post and over the wall to freedom. One night, the safe house in which Hamill and Kerrigan were staying was raided by the Branch following a tip-off, and the pair, being veteran escapers, tried to make a getaway through the back door. After a quick shoot-out they realised they were surrounded and the situation was hopeless. They were outmanned, outgunned and outwitted. Hamill spent a short stint in Arbour Hill prison before he was deposited in the Curragh for the remainder of the war.

Some of the Derry escapees were ordered by the IRA to sign themselves out of the Curragh by undertaking not to return to the struggle, an act that was deemed hugely dishonourable by hardline republicans. They were to return to the beleaguered struggle north of the border, where one of them, Rocky Burns, was installed as OC in Belfast. In February 1944, Burns and an unarmed companion from the South were passing by the back of the GPO in Belfast on their way to Royal Avenue. Two detectives stopped them and asked for identity cards, then one of them lifted Burns's hat and said, 'That's our man.' They were arrested and taken in the direction of Queen's Street barracks. As they approached the barracks, Burns produced a gun and shot at the detectives, who returned fire aided by another armed officer who had come out of the barracks. In the mêlée his companion got clean away, but Burns dropped to the ground clutching his stomach. He died two days later at the age of twenty-three.

Of the twenty-one escapees, the only success story was Brendan O'Boyle, who made it scot-free to the United States, the land of liberty. On returning home in 1955, he founded Laochra Uladh, a small republican group bent on a bombing campaign in the North. Dressed as a very convincing Yankee tourist, he made his way to the Stormont parliament whilst it was closed. He explained to the security guard that his dear old Dad had worked on the construction of the building before emigrating to the States. When O'Boyle slipped the guard a crisp fifty-pound note, he was allowed through to take photographs of the building, and set about reconnoitring the impressive façade. He told the guard that his wife, who was out shopping, would also wish to see the great building, so he scheduled another day to return for further photographs, with the promise of another £50 note. A couple of days later O'Boyle returned with a bomb cunningly disguised as a large camera case. As he was preparing it, it exploded prematurely, killing him instantly.

The Derry escape was the IRA's last great propaganda coup of the forties and gave the slumping movement a temporary jab in the arm, despite only three escapees managing to evade recapture for any considerable length of time. Buoyed by the escape, the IRA shortly afterwards decided on another propaganda coup, to commemorate the Easter Rising by taking over the Broadway cinema, on Belfast's Falls Road, on Easter Sunday. The area was awash with RUC men bent on preventing illegal Rising commemorations, but the cinema was one place they had overlooked. Armed volunteers were stationed at the doors, on the roof, and across the street from the picture house. The film *Don Bosco* had the packed house enthralled, but the excitement of the picture was to pale in comparison to what was about to happen. The volunteers moved. The film projector was taken over and a slide placed in front of it which lit up the screen: 'This cinema has been commandeered by the Irish Republican Army for the purpose of holding an Easter commemoration ...' The proclamation was read out by Jimmy Steele and a statement from the Army Council was read by the Chief of Staff, Hugh McAteer, to thunderous applause: 'Now with Britain engaged in a struggle for her very existence, we are presented with a glorious opportunity…' The time was ripe to raise the flag in the fourth green field but the take-over of the Broadway cinema proved to be one of the last puffs of life from a beaten organisation that had, by this time, over a thousand members firmly behind bars, North and South.

The general feeling among the escapees was that they were badly let down by the IRA on the outside and many regretted that they hadn't tried to get away on their own. The escape had been ill-timed too, and many thought that a night-time escape would have yielded a higher success rate in spite of the curfew. Few of the escapees had anticipated their reception in the Free State and were genuinely sur-prised to be re-interned south of the border.

When the forties campaign finally fizzled out, the majority of the Derry escapees returned to civilian life. After his release from the Curragh, the former prison adjutant and one of the leaders of the escape, Jimmy O'Hagan, was reunited with his wife and child and they tried to settle in Dublin. They set off to find a job and a flat as his wife, May, had been struggling on her own and things were getting quite desperate. They had finally found a nice landlady who would rent them a place, but she sent them packing when the young Pierce O'Hagan boasted to her, 'My Daddy escaped from prison.'

Breaking the Waves

THE FIRST BOAT THAT PADDY ADAMS ever set foot on was HMS *Maidstone*, a prison ship in Belfast Lough. All 100,000 tons of this ex-naval ship sat in the murky water of the Musgrave Channel, stretching nearly five hundred feet from fore to aft. She was launched on Clydebank in 1937 with the words 'May God bless you and all who sail in you.' As Adams walked gingerly up the gangway, the handrail of which was wrapped in coils of barbed wire, he wondered if this blessing also extended to him. Only forty-eight hours previously he had been walking through his home estate of Bally-murphy, in West Belfast, when a British army Saracen came speeding through the streets. A sixth sense told him to turn into a friend's house instead of going home, but as he was doing so the Brits came in behind him, arrested him, threw him into the back of the Saracen and took him off to Holy-wood interrogation centre in County Down. It was inevitable that he would be lifted, coming as he did from an ardently republican family. His uncle Paddy, after whom he was named, was one of the twenty-one who had escaped from Derry prison in 1943.

In Holywood barracks Adams was deprived of sleep and

beaten whilst under interrogation, but having met with no success during his questioning the authorities dispatched the relieved Adams to the *Maidstone*. On arrival, he was given a cursory medical examination by the prison doctor, at which he was deemed fit, and sent to join the other internees. He descended the steep stairs to the prisoners' interior deck to be greeted by friends and neighbours who had already been lifted, among them his good mate Harry Burns. His tortuous journey was over, but his motionless voyage had just begun.

▲▲▲

At 4.00am on 9 August 1971, Operation Demetrius had been put into effect and three hundred and forty-two known republicans were arrested and interned. Internment essentially meant imprisonment without trial until the authorities decided whether you were a threat to the state or not. The clanking sound of dustbin lids on flagstones rang out across the Catholic ghettos of West Belfast. The women of the estate used it as an alarm, to signal that the British troops were coming into the estate to round up their men-folk. The trouble on the streets had been, with each passing week, escalating more and more, and the Stormont government was losing control of the situation. As the disorder had worsened and the IRA had begun to regroup in the North, the unionists had clamoured for the re-introduction of internment. It had worked in the twenties, forties, and fifties; it would surely work again in the seventies.

Instead of calming the street disorder, however, the government's policy of lifting men from only one side in the sectarian divide in the North increased the mayhem. The British army was acting on poor Stormont intelligence, which was often outmoded or entirely incorrect. Many of the Provos were tipped off about the pre-dawn swoop by spies in Stormont and made themselves scarce. The operation degenerated into a shambles and more often than not uninvolved sons or brothers of former activists were lifted and interned for no apparent reason. In addition, internment took out the older generation of activists who could have exercised control over the younger generation. The violence intensified as a result, and it is now thought that the government's policy of internment was actually the best recruiting incentive that the IRA could have hoped for. Such was the clamour to sign up that the IRA had to turn away potential members and organise itself into smaller and more cohesive groups.

As more and more people were being arrested for street disturbances, and still more were being lifted for internment, the logistics of housing these prisoners reached emergency proportions. A factory site in Antrim was considered as a possible location but was deemed inappropriate as a centre of detention and so a clandestine plan was put into operation. It was decided that the old wartime airfield at Long Kesh, near Lisburn, could be hastily renovated along the lines of a prisoner-of-war camp for the internees. Publicly, it was announced that the renovation was to accommodate the swelling numbers of British troops in the province, and all the work was carried out by army staff. In reality the plan involved installing fencing and watch towers, concealing until the last moment the real reason for the transformation of the site into a fortress. However, the internee accommodation crisis worsened before the completion of the camp and, as time was in short supply, the authorities were forced to consider other options.

One obvious solution was to surround the internees with natural impediments to escaping, and a number of offshore islands were considered. The authorities considered sending them to the Isle of Man, but special legislation would be required to remove internees from the province. Rathlin Island, off the North Antrim coast, was also considered but ruled out for logistical reasons. The only other short-term option left was a prison ship. There is a long history of holding republicans on prison ships, the first two being the *Postlethwaite* and the *William and James*, which were moored in Belfast lough during the rebellion of 1798. In January of that year, one prisoner by the name of Cassidy made a bid for freedom and tried to swim ashore. He was easily targeted by the sentries on duty and was shot dead, sinking to a watery grave.

As history was to witness, these floating prisons were perhaps the most escape-proof means of housing prisoners. They were the Northern equivalent of Alcatraz. The *Argenta* housed republican internees in the 1920s, and the *Al Rawdah* was the floating home of internees during World War II. Nobody had ever escaped alive from any of these four ships. The conditions on the prison ships had been appalling, and the authorities were concerned about the negative propaganda possibilities of such a move. By this stage Crumlin Road jail was dangerously full, housing some nine hundred prisoners, and the authorities were faced with no other choice but to opt for a sea-borne vessel as a short-term solution. They considered bringing the old frigate ship HMS *Belfast* home to the city of its birth to house the detainees, but its design left it prone to sabotage – the ship's services, such as water and electricity, ran from stern to aft and could easily be tampered with by the prisoners.

The old depot ship, HMS *Maidstone*, which was already being used as an emergency billet for British soldiers since 1969, did not have this design flaw and, after some hasty renovation, was moored in Belfast Lough adjacent to the Harland and Wolff jetty at Kelly's coalyard. She was listed as a nuclear support ship in admiralty records, as she had supported the nuclear submarine HMS *Dreadnought*. In 1969 she had been wrapped in mothballs in preparation for dismantling, but when trouble erupted in Northern Ireland she was given a temporary reprieve from the scrapyard. She was now the home to over six hundred British army officers. On her transformation into a prison ship, three decks were isolated for internees – two for living quarters and the top deck as an exercise deck. On each of the interior decks there were recreational areas, bathrooms with open showers, and a kitchen. Two- and three-tier bunk beds lined each wall of the living quarters, and it was not long before they were filled with over one hundred and fifty internees from Newry, Derry, Tyrone and Armagh, transferred there by helicopter in batches of six, all handcuffed together. The local Belfast internees soon joined them.

▲▲▲

Tommy Gorman was a member of the IRA's first battalion, E Company, in Andersonstown, who specialised in bank jobs. But their OC, Sean Convery, was lifted in September of 1971 and deposited in Crumlin Road jail. They had to spring him, and so Gorman, with Tucker Kane, another IRA man, were sent to reconnoitre the prison surroundings dressed as officials from the council. They looked the part with their clipboards and stamps of officialdom, and under the auspices of investigating complaints of a rat infestation the two 'council men' inspected the houses that ran along the back of the prison. An elderly occupant of one of the houses spotted the two mooching around the yard and approached them. They explained to him what they were doing. 'Rats!' he exclaimed, 'that's the least of our problems. Look at the bloody damp in this house.' He had been waiting all his life to lay his hands on a council official, and he wasn't going to let this opportunity pass. He made the two some tea, and when he was assured of a captive audience, he tore strips off them over his poor treatment by the council. The two took copious notes of what the man was saying and were relieved when he finally ran out of complaints. They hurriedly left the area before another householder got his hands on them.

Gorman and Kane investigated different options for the escape and finally settled on the simplest, that of lobbing rope ladders over the perimeter wall at a time when the warders would be most distracted. It was pretty basic, but effective. Having studied the warders' behaviour over a period, those on the inside thought that this escape plan could be executed successfully, provided it was timed correctly. As more and more prisoners arrived in 'The Crum', as the jail was known, the authorities needed more space for the prisoners' recreational facilities, and the new all-weather soccer pitch was located very close to the perimeter wall.

This was chosen as the place for the escape, for the prisoners could simply abandon their game and clamber over the wall before the warders knew what was happening.

Following communication from the inside, 11.00am on 16 November was selected as zero hour. Gorman and Kane arrived on the Cliftonpark Avenue side of the jail. From the other side of the wall they could hear the sounds of fevered activity, the panting and cursing of an intense football match that was being played. From the wings, the warders watched on, bored. It wasn't much of a game for the spectators but the participants were relishing it. They were going over the wall. Eleven of them, just enough for a soccer team, had been selected to mount the wall while another fifteen were detailed to prevent the prison officers from stopping them. At 11.10am, during the second half, two rope ladders were thrown over the perimeter wall by Gorman and Kane. Kane climbed up one and sat on the wall with a gun in his hand, waiting for firing from the British army post. None came. Not needing any further invitation, the 'Crumlin Kangaroos', as they were later known, clambered up the ropes like army recruits, mounting the high wall. There was total bedlam. The warders were outnumbered but did manage to regain control after nine prisoners had escaped. When the escapees landed on the far side, they made their way into the getaway cars. As they sped to the safe houses, they took off their soccer gear and donned normal civilian clothing, disappearing into the streets of Belfast.

Five days later, a British army patrol stopped a car containing four Cistercian monks as it crossed the border into the South. They looked holier than thou. The policeman checked their papers, which seemed genuine, but on closer examination he discovered that two of the hooded men were the fugitives Danny Mullan and Christopher Keenan, both Crumlin Kangaroos. The other seven escapees made it to Sinn Féin's Dublin headquarters for a press conference the following week, having enjoyed the traditional right of sanctuary with the Cistercians in Tyrone. For Gorman and Kane the escape was a great success, except for the fact that Sean Convery, the man they'd meant to spring, was still on the inside. He had failed to get over the wall.

▲▲▲

Two months later, on 27 December 1971, Tucker Kane and Tommy Gorman were staying with Peter Rodgers in a house in Lenadoon when they were all lifted and brought to a basement cell in the barracks on Blacks Road. There they were confronted with a number of blankets with eyeholes cut in them, through which peered beady little eyes. 'Yes, that's them,' said the mysterious figure, and so the following day they were brought to Holywood interrogation centre. It wasn't long before Gorman was re-united with his OC, for after three days' rough treatment in Holywood he and his comrades joined Convery on the *Maidstone* on the very first day of 1972. All of them had been born with an excess of the escape gene, and the first thing they set their minds to was a bid for freedom. After all, as internees, they hadn't been given a release date. Conceivably you could be locked up forever.

Internment continued apace, and it was clear from the ragbag of internees on the *Maidstone* that one didn't necessarily have to be a republican to be lifted. There were many there who had never worn an Easter lily in their lives, be it stick-on or pin-up. One innocent man was driven to dementia at being detained and spent most of his time shouting into a disused tube on the boat: 'Abandon ship! Abandon ship!' Another internee, Hugh Elliot, had simply been going for a pint in St John's Club in Ballymurphy when his cousin Jimmy asked him to help out his wife, who was getting a hard time from the paratroopers. Jimmy was stopped by the paras, and when asked his name, replied 'Mickey Mouse', in a thick Belfast accent. Turning to Hugh, the para asked, 'What's your name, then?' 'Donald Duck,' Hugh shot back. 'All right, Duckie, you're on your way to Disneyland,' and so Hugh ended up winning a one-way cruise on the prison ship *Maidstone*.

If some of the internees didn't quite know what they were doing there, the same could be said for some of the prison officers. Many were ex-army officers recruited from England, simply filling in their time and drawing a wage packet. The rest were locally employed officers, and were a little more vigilant in patrolling the boat, but a cunning propaganda campaign by the internees soon saw them become as *laissez-faire* as the others. The internees had noticed that the imported officers were being paid more than the local boys, and had posted the recruitment advertisements around the deck which displayed the differences in pay. This had the desired psychological effect and the local boys lost their vigilance and became equally inattentive.

Security on the *Maidstone* itself was the responsibility of the prison officers, but the physical security of the surrounding area came under British army control. The nearby jetty was covered by a sandbagged army emplacement, and there were numerous armed observation posts both on and off the ship to prevent an escape bid. The army had sunk coils of barbed wire and sensor devices on the outer perimeter of the boat to deter any prospective swimmers, the surrounding water was floodlit by night and there was an extensive no-go area for boats in the vicinity of the prison ship. It seemed that there simply was no way out.

Because they were very poor swimmers, which meant that escape on the open-water side of the boat was not an option, Paddy Adams and Harry Burns concentrated their efforts on escaping from the dry-dock side. The internees were permitted one hour's exercise on the top deck each day, and the two boys scoured the surrounding area for a potential escape route or vehicle. They could see that on these dark winter nights a thick fog would descend over the lough, which would give good cover in spite of the floodlights. They also observed that one of the steel hawsers that moored the boat swung very near one of the portholes to which they had access in the prisoners' quarters. If they could cut the bars on the porthole they could use a sweeping brush to hook on to the hawser nearest them, climb out, use their belts to slide down to the dock below and make off into the wild grey yonder. It was possible, but even if you did make it to the dock you were only half-way there and sure to be discovered before getting any further. They required a means of getting from the bottom of the hawser to the other side of the army compound without detection. So it was back to the drawing board.

They asked one of the internees, who was due a visit from

his mother, to ask her for a razor blade in order that they could get started on the bars. On the visit, as subtly as possible, he asked his Ma for the blades, but she replied 'Sure what do you want blades for, son, you don't even shave!' and the conversation moved on. Then one day whilst they were exercising on deck, Adams and Burns got word that a parcel had arrived for them, always an occasion they relished. They opened the parcel to discover a wooden box, made from floorboards, which was divided into three compartments. In the first there were Woodbine cigarettes, the second contained Park Drive cigarettes and the third held a huge packet of raspberry ruffles. As lads just out of their teens, they were particularly pleased with the ruffles. While the fags were distributed among the smokers, the two boys tucked into the ruffles and the wooden box was cast into the bin where it fell apart. On closer examination the boys could just see a hacksaw blade emerging from a groove in the box. It was stealthily appropriated and hidden for potentially invaluable future use.

With each passing day and new arrival, Adams and Burns were beginning to think that they had more friends on the boat than on dry land. Their friend and neighbour, big Jim Bryson, arrived as an internee and after they had exchanged formalities, he asked the lads had they got the hacksaw blades he had sent in. Up until then they had no idea who their benefactor had been. Like them, Bryson had no intention of staying on the boat any longer than he had to. The next Ballymurphy man to be dispatched to the boat was Tommy 'Todler' Toland, who similarly was in no mood to wait for his release papers. In addition to their drive to escape, Toland and Bryson had the advantage of being able to swim. With them, Burns, Adams, Tommy Gorman and Tucker Kane formed an escape think-tank and they brain-stormed through dozens of potential escape plans.

▲▲▲

As they'd already decided, the landward side of the boat was a non-starter. It was too heavily guarded and an escape would entail significant outside help and considerable risk. The initial plan for the dockside was adaptable to the other side of the ship, though. They had heard a rumour that there was an electrical sensor that would set off an alarm if there were any movement around the boat. As they were talking all the possibilities through on deck, they spotted a seal swimming nearby. Gorman rushed to get a piece of meat and tossed it into the sea, teasing the seal between the wires to where they thought the sensor device was. Enticed by the meat, the seal glided around the wires. There was no alarm! That was the way out. The only tricky part was getting beyond the coils of barbed wire that surrounded the boat, but they figured they could swing out beyond it. The think-tank cast around for other swimmers, strong enough to make the five hundred yards across the channel to the Harland and Wolff shipyard on the far shore. The escape required a degree of bravado and it was Gorman who suggested the other three names: Sean Convery (his former OC), Martin Taylor and Peter Rodgers. They joined the original four: Tucker Kane, Tommy Toland, Tommy Gorman and Jim Bryson. For some of these chosen few, time was running out. As prisoners were often transferred off the ship to a jail on land with little or no warning, speed was of the essence as any or all of them could be moved at any moment.

As with all escapes, the plan was straightforward; the execution was the difficult part. Their Echo margarine rations and boot polish were stored up to smear on the swimmers' bodies: the margarine was to insulate them from the cold, the boot polish was to make them less visible to the British army sentry post. They would wait for the foggiest night, cut the two diagonal steel bars that blocked the port-hole, and a scout's lift would see the lads up and through the port-hole to the other side. Then came the dangerous part. They had to hook a sweeping brush around a rope that hung on that side of the boat, and use it to swing beyond the coils of barbed wire and out into the sea below. If they mistimed it and got entangled in the barbed wire, they were sure to be pulled under. Of great concern was the fact that they would hit the water with a splash, which was sure to attract the unwanted attention of the sentry post. It was worth the risk, though. On landing in the murky water, the priority was to minimise the noise so all were instructed to swim the breaststroke underwater and after gaining some distance, to come up for air and submerge again. Then all that was left was the five hundred yards to shore which, even with the currents, they were all confident they could achieve if they took their time.

In mid-January, the water was bound to be ice-cold. There was a limit to how long they could survive in such freezing conditions. Night after night they watched the city's rubbish floating past, caught in the currents on the lough. There was quite a tug in some patches and they agreed that if any one of them got into difficulty they wouldn't call out as this would jeopardise the escape for the others – they could all be shot. It was make or break, sink or swim. For the days prior to the escape bid, the boys embarked on a rigorous training routine to prepare for this, the swim of their lives. They freaked one another out with talk of the paras shooting to kill or legendary shark attacks. Cold showers were endured to acclimatise themselves to the chilly waters – that was Tucker Kane's suggestion. In the shower next to Kane, Tommy Gorman stood underneath the bracing cold shower for as long as he could bear it. It felt like the icy water was almost burning a hole through him. From the shower next to him he could hear the gasps and pants of Kane breaking the pain threshold as the cold water blasted him. Judging by the sound of Kane's breathing, he seemed to be suffering badly, so Gorman popped his head around to check up on him. There was Kane shaking like a leaf, every breath gasped out as if it were his last, but he was dry as a bone. The bastard had the shower head pointing at the wall! On seeing Gorman, he burst out laughing.

Crucial to the escape plan was the creation of an atmosphere of normality on the deck, behind which the plotters could work unnoticed. The internees formed a skiffle group, playing combs, *bodhráns* and tin whistles as they belted out Johnny Duncan and Lonnie Donegan numbers with gusto. They rehearsed strategically close to the porthole. Others were stationed nearby, playing chess and draughts in order to block any investigation by the prison officers. As the escapees waited for that elusive night of dense fog to arrive, they thought they were scuppered by a supply ship which was moored on the lough side of the *Maidstone*, preventing their descent into the water. But fortune was favouring them, for this ship enabled them to see the positions of the British army guards on the upper decks by the shadows they cast on its hull. They waited until the guard's shadow was directly above the porthole, then threw large cans of water into the lough below, which crashed through the surface. No reaction. The para could neither see nor hear any evil, nor would he speak of it. There was a shining steel hawser suspended from the *Maidstone*'s top deck which was used to moor the two ships together, draped tantalisingly beyond the barbed wire as if pointing the way out. There would be no need for any rope-swinging or splashing into the water now. Word came through from the officers that some of the detainees were to be moved. The names were called, and some of those who were in on the escape were given their marching orders. It was like an execution notice.

Two days later, a thick fog was forecast and the seven swimmers were in readiness. Word of the escape bid was smuggled out and an armed IRA unit from Andersonstown was to meet them on the other side of the dock, with two cars and, more importantly, warm clothes for the partially naked swimmers. The timing was crucial. The routine on the boat was that the warders would perform a head count after the prisoners had had their tea. They wouldn't be counted again until that evening, so this would maximise their time spent undetected. The count would be over by 4.00pm and this was chosen as the time for the escape. Darkness would have descended by then and their landing on the far shore would coincide with the shipyard workers finishing their shifts. Donning the clothes supplied by the IRA welcoming unit, they would simply mingle with the crowds returning to the city.

BREAK-OUT!

▲▲▲

As the afternoon light faded on 17 January 1972, the anticipated fog crept in from the lough and enveloped the boat like
a clammy skin. The water was eerily still, glass-like. Too still,
almost. The fog brought with it a quietness that lingered in the
frosty air. The only sound was the constant, relentless drone
of the *Maidstone*'s engines. Any other sound seemed to reverberate through the night, no doubt exaggerated to the escapees' hyper-alert ears. After their tea, the warders started the
head count but the numbers didn't tally. They were one short.
Alarm set in among the escapees but they kept their cool until
the missing inmate was found on the toilet, in blissful igno-
rance of the rising panic. The count started all over again,
delaying the lads' departure. Shit! This would affect the timing
of the rest of the plan. Would the boys still be there to greet
them on the far side? Would they be too late for the Harland
and Wolff workers? As they were only half an hour behind,
they decided to proceed anyway.

The next thing to do was to begin cutting the port-hole
bars without alerting the warders. The eight warders on duty,
who mingled with the internees, always stayed in pairs and
the internees now did their utmost to distract their attention.
A game of cards or a chat about the racing results would suf-
fice as most of the warders were just putting in their time,
waiting for their shift to end. If they did notice anything afoot
at the porthole, there were volunteers assigned to restrain
them by force. As soon as the hacksaw blade began cutting
into the porthole's steel bars, the skiffle sing-song started and
the record player jumped into life. But to the warders, it was
like any other day, indeed every other day. In contrast, all

the internees were caught up in the excitement of the build-up, with the exception of one, John O'Donoghue, who slept through all the commotion despite his bunk being adjacent to the escapees' porthole.

Harry Burns started the sawing; it didn't quite cut like a hot knife through Echo margarine, but after persistent hacking the bar gave way. He bent it upwards and outwards to the stars. It then occurred to Burns that with just one bar cut there would be enough room for a man to wriggle through sideways. He came down from the porthole beaming from ear to ear and turned to the escapees. It was a go! The seven men were smeared from head to foot in margarine and boot polish, like minstrels gone wrong. The only items of clothing they wore were black underpants and socks on their hands and feet, to protect them from lacerations on the steel hawser. Bryson turned to Adams and said: 'Come on out, you.' 'But I'm terrified of the water,' came the reply. 'I'll knock you out, put two cartons around you and float you over,' Bryson offered. Thanks, but no thanks, thought Adams and he vowed that, as soon as he got off this boat, he was going to learn to swim.

First out was Tommy Gorman, a powerful swimmer. Fuelled by adrenalin, he was given a scout's lift and wriggled his body through the porthole. The first thing that struck him was the cold wintry air on his naked skin. As he hooked the hawser into his grasp the water below seemed to him to be very brightly lit. He was sure the sentries would see him. He figured he could lower himself halfway, and then haul himself up if the coast wasn't clear. As his greasy hands gripped the hawser, he realised this was the point of no return and slid all the way down to the water. He hit the surface like a gannet, sank down and started the breaststroke, terrified to break the surface in case a hail of bullets from the paras would greet him.

After swimming about fifty yards and desperate for air, he burst to the surface on his back and looked back towards the ship. To him it seemed as bright as day on the water. To the others on the boat waiting to jump in, he also looked disturbingly visible. Gorman looked towards the British army post but there was nothing stirring. He savoured the moment a little longer before he kicked himself underwater again and made for land. When he surfaced the second time he looked back towards the ship. Where were his comrades? Was he the only one in the water? He could see the other internees back on the boat waving and gesturing. Was this an elaborate prank? Had nobody else followed him, or had they been caught on the inside? At this stage, he thought himself sufficiently far from the boat to start the crawl. Perhaps it was the margarine, or maybe just raw adrenalin, but he didn't feel the cold, nor did he feel tired. When he made it to the far shore after a twenty-five minute swim, he hauled himself from the water and looked around for the welcoming party. They were nowhere to be seen, so he hid beneath a small quay where coal was being unloaded for the nearby power station. He hugged his knees close to him, awaiting the arrival of the others. It was only then that the freezing air started to really bite.

The others *had* gone into the water, however, and were crossing the channel with varying degrees of success. Midway across, where the current was strongest, Convery was running out of steam and Toland swam over to assist him and get him back into his stride. Rodgers too ran into troubled waters, as fighting the current was wearing him out. He turned on his back and tried the backstroke, glancing up from time to time to ensure he was on course, when suddenly from the corner of his eye he spied a patrol boat. But it turned out to be a harmless buoy, but this was just the jolt he required to regain his energies and make it to the shore.

Back on the boat, Harry Burns was delighted with himself: he had lifted all seven men out the porthole to freedom. The only tricky one was big Jim Bryson, who needed a bit of a push to squeeze through the gap. This was great job satisfaction! He looked around in triumph only to see John O'Donoghue, still sound asleep. A passing herd of bison would not awaken him. All those in on the escape bid watched the swimmers' progress across the channel until they disappeared into the fog. They could scarcely hide their glee and it was time to wind up the warders. 'How's that game of Monopoly going?' 'I wouldn't throw away that bishop if I were you.' A full hour and a half passed before the officers realised what had happened. When they found the porthole, the soldiers were called in to round up all the internees, bringing them into the canteen for a head count.

The prisoners overheard the senior officer saying that there were eight escapees. The boys looked at each other in confusion. Had somebody made an unofficial bid for freedom? For about ten minutes they were scouring the boat to see who it was that had gone, when out came a sleepy John O'Donoghue yawning and rubbing his eyes asking what all the fuss was about. Only seven had got away. One was dreaming of it. 'What's your name?' a warder asked one of the internees during the head count. 'Jim Bryson,' came the reply. By the end of the head count there were three Jim Brysons on the boat, and the soldiers had to resort to checking their internment files to ascertain the identity of the missing men. This would afford the escapees valuable time before their details could be circulated for identification.

▲▲▲

One of Belfast's bus drivers, who worked the route that ran from the Harland and Wolff dockyard to the estates of East Belfast, had just completed his round and was returning to the terminus at the docks for his next departure. In these troubled times, there was always tight security within the shipyard and the entrance was blocked by a barrier. When the security guard saw the bus driver he lifted the barrier and let him through with a friendly nod. The driver parked at the bus stop and waited for his next departure time. It was now past six o'clock, and at this stage most of the workers were already at home tucking into their dinner. This late departure was to facilitate overtime staff.

As he sat there in the empty bus, he was stunned to see a semi-naked man jump on. Wearing nothing but his underpants and socks and smeared with black streaks, the shivering stranger said, 'I've fallen off a ship and had to swim ashore. Can you get me to a hospital?' He explained that his clothes had been dragging him down and he had to take them off. The driver tried to calm the blackened stranger as much as he could. The best thing for this guy to do was to get to the security hut where they would look after him, but he wouldn't go and kept moaning about getting to a hospital because he was at risk from hypothermia. The driver offered him his coat, which he gratefully accepted. There was something very suspicious about this whole situation so the driver insisted that they go to the security guards. Then the weird stranger turned on him, hitting him so hard that the driver was knocked to the ground by the blow. What was wrong with this guy? The stranger made off, but then turned towards him again, reached into the pockets of the jacket that the driver had just given him, took out all the money, and threw it at him. Tommy Gorman then turned on his heels back to the coal jetty. He didn't want the bus driver to think he was a crook. Utterly bewildered, the driver picked himself up, started the bus, and headed off on his round, wondering why some of these characters were allowed to roam the streets.

Gorman made his way to the pier and found that five of the lads had gathered there, some of them now completely naked. Where was Convery? They waited and waited, even considering swimming back towards the *Maidstone* to see if he was struggling, but finally decided they couldn't delay any longer and needed to get warm. So they went in search of transport, as their welcoming party had obviously left already. Across the road, near the huge Harland and Wolff cranes, was a yellow Vauxhall Viva that had been left unlocked, so the six semi-naked men piled in, out of the piercing wind, and tried to collect their thoughts. They kept as low as possible, being a queer sight for any passer-by. Rodgers set about hotwiring the car, but his hands were the colour of the wiring and he couldn't manage it.

Gorman informed them of the bus he had seen, and they

realised that this could be their ticket out. Suddenly Convery, who had had the most difficulty swimming, arrived and the magnificent seven were united again. After a quick consultation they decided to try and hijack the bus that Gorman had told them about. Rodgers whipped the woolly seat cover from the Vauxhall and wrapped it around himself, while Jim Bryson found an umbrella, and a bowler hat which fitted him quite snugly, then they raced off down the pier. Behind them came Gorman, who looked for all the world like a flasher with his naked legs protruding from underneath his long busman's coat. In varying states of undress, the others brought up the rear, their wet socks trailing as they ran towards the bus, which by this time had been into the city and back again. The seven lads hugged the shadows, like poorly paid extras in a low-budget zombie movie.

There was nobody on the bus when they got there, as the driver had probably gone to security to report the earlier incident. Peter Rodgers, who had been a bus driver before he was lifted, leapt into the driver's seat. The keys were still in the ignition. Just then, the bus driver returned with two security guards and jumped on the bus to stop what appeared to be a hijack. He came face to face with another semi-naked lunatic. Tucker Kane punched him in the jaw and he fell off the bus into the arms of the security guards. Rodgers roared the bus into life. This scene was witnessed by a number of other security guards, who jumped into a grey security van that was parked nearby and set off in pursuit. They notified the front gate about the hijack as they knew that the bus could be trapped inside the compound.

The security man at the front gate was pre-warned so that

when he saw the bus approaching, he came out and raised his hand aloft to stop it. It was gaining speed. He realised that these guys weren't stopping, and he dived out of the way as the bus crashed through the main gates. On the bus, Tommy Toland and Jim Bryson sat in the middle aisle singing rebel songs at the tops of their voices while Rodgers pushed the bus to its capacity, slamming the gears and leaning on the accelerator. He wanted to get to West Belfast, but they would never make it in this bus as the RUC were now in pursuit. By looking out the back window, the others could tell Rodgers which side their pursuers were trying to overtake on, and he would lunge from side to side to block them. He decided to head for the nearest nationalist area, the Markets. He crossed the Lagan at Queen's bridge, turned down Oxford Street and into the Markets, up Cromac Street and into Verner Street. They'd never follow us in here, he thought as he pulled up outside a pub, and the seven rushed inside. The local kids started to dismantle the bus like piranha fish.

Inside the pub, when the punters heard where the seven naked strangers had come from they took off their shirts and trousers and offered them to the escapees, who all donned ill-fitting jackets and shoes. One man handed them the keys to his car and they sped off to safe houses in Andersonstown, but before going into hiding Tommy Gorman paid a brief, but risky, visit home to his heavily pregnant wife. While the RUC were still searching the Markets, kicking in doors and holding suspected safe-house owners for detention, the escapees were all safely billeted around the city, and the following Friday they were smuggled across the border, where a press conference was held to mark the escape of the 'Magnificent Seven'. Back on the *Maidstone* the internees settled down to watch the early-evening news. There, from an undisclosed location in Dublin, their seven former shipmates were paraded in front of the world's press. The roof nearly came off the deck with the jubilant din. HMS *Maidstone* was closed on 9 April 1972 and she was sent to Scotland for scrapping.

Tucker Kane and Martin Taylor were recaptured in May of the same year, while Gorman and Bryson remained at large until September. Of all the escapees Bryson was the toughest *hombre*, and he would patrol the Ballymurphy estate armed with his favourite weapon, a Lewis machine-gun, in the hope of encountering and engaging with a British army patrol. He was a lethal sniper who relished combat. Nine months after the *Maidstone* escape he was arrested for possession of a weapon and held in Long Kesh internment camp while awaiting trial. When his day in court was drawing near, he was transferred to Crumlin Road jail as it was directly across the road from Belfast's courthouse. In an ingenious piece of architectural design, there was a tunnel beneath the Crumlin Road connecting the jail to the courthouse. This served a two-fold purpose: firstly, prisoners could be kept out of sight and therefore out of mind, and secondly, prisoners could be escorted to court underground without the expense and security risk of transfer in a prison van.

On the morning of his trial, 22 February 1973, Bryson was led from the jail to the courthouse along with three others. Unbeknownst to the prison officer escorting him he was in possession of a small .25 hand-gun. The gun had been smuggled into the jail and Bryson had commandeered it for his own escape bid. The prisoners were being deposited in the cells below the courthouse, to await their call to trial, when Bryson turned on the warder and pulled his gun. The warder was ordered to strip and was tied up in the cell. Bryson donned his clothes and made his way out the front door of the courthouse, an officer in uniform. Cleverly he made his way to the nearby loyalist Shankill Road, where he flagged down a car, beseeching its occupants to take him to the Royal Victoria hospital, pretending that he had just got word that his wife had gone into labour. Belfast's Royal Victoria is conveniently located close to the heartland of nationalist West Belfast. Republican legend has it that these unwitting Samaritans were off-duty UDR soldiers.

Bryson later crossed the border into the South, thus making good his second escape in thirteen months. However, Bryson's personality was one that was not going to lie low for too long. He was more likely to burn out than to fade away, and he soon returned to Ballymurphy to resume the struggle. On 31 August 1973 he was on an assignment with volunteer Paddy Mulvenna and two others. As they waited in a car, a covert unit of British army paratroopers opened fire on them from an empty flat above a row of shops. The twenty-two-year-old Mulvenna was killed instantly, but Jim Bryson survived another three weeks, dying as a result of his injuries at the age of twenty-five. He is immortalised in a mural on the gable wall of a Ballymurphy house wielding his weapon of choice, the Lewis machine-gun. Another of his *Maidstone* escape comrades, Tommy Toland, is similarly immortalised in Ballymurphy. He was executed in 1977 in a vicious internecine dispute between the Provisional and the Official IRA, one of four lives the feud took that day. Tucker Kane died on active service in a particularly horrific car accident on the Glen Road, West Belfast, in July 1976.

Of the seven escapees, only four are left alive to tell their story. Peter Rodgers was sentenced to eighteen years in Portlaoise prison for killing Garda Seamus Quaid in a quarry in Ballyconnick, County Wexford. Four years into his sentence, along with two of the Maze escapees, he made another escape bid. During Mass on Sunday, 24 November 1984, Rodgers produced a gun and held the prison staff hostage. Along with eleven other IRA men, he dressed in prison-officer uniform and planned to make his way out of the prison, but as the twelve were passing through the first security gate, it swung shut and Rodgers was trapped on the inside. The other eleven men passed through six of the gates with the help of forged keys. Using smuggled explosives, they tried to blow a hole in a steel door, but it was too strong – it dented but didn't open. They gave themselves up. Rodgers was released at the end of 1998 under the Good Friday Agreement, and now lives in Belfast, as do Tommy Gorman and Sean Convery. The last of the escapees, Martin Taylor, now lives in the west of Ireland where he works, in an ironic twist of fate, as a locksmith.

The Birdmen of Mountjoy

IT WAS HALLOWEEN IN 1973, and Rosaleen Twomey was making her twice-weekly visit from Belfast to Dublin's Mountjoy jail to visit her husband, Seamus. He had been arrested six weeks previously by Inspector John McMenamin in Carrickmacross, County Monaghan, and was handed down a sentence of five years for membership of the IRA and for handling stolen cash, the proceeds of an armed robbery in Kerry. He had been locked up for the previous three weeks in the notorious Victorian prison's D wing, which was reserved for republican prisoners and now housed eighty-two. The republicans considered D wing their natural home. It was there that O'Donovan Rossa had been held, as well as the Land League prisoners, so they were in good company in this God-forsaken place.

Mrs Twomey had known when she married this ardent republican that these times would inevitably come. When they married in 1948, he had only been two years at liberty. He had spent the previous seven as an internee, incarcerated at the behest of His Majesty during the Second World War. As Rosaleen rounded the corner of Dublin's North Circular Road and proceeded down the short stretch to fortress Mountjoy, she reflected that she was no stranger to prisons herself. Her own brother was one of the last to be whipped with the cat o' nine tails in Belfast prison, while she herself had been imprisoned from 1942 to 1945, in Armagh jail, for her part in a bank robbery in West Belfast's Balaclava Street; the irony that she might have got away with it, had she been wearing a balaclava at the time, was not lost on her. She waited patiently for her husband to appear. The prison officer arrived, and said bluntly, 'He doesn't want to see you.' She was taken aback. 'What?' she asked. 'Yeah, he says you have had a row.' She was racking her brains for something she might have said to upset him. Had she neglected an anniversary? Despite her entreaties, the officer said that Seamus refused point blank to see her. She left the prison dismayed and headed back to Belfast. Still puzzling over her husband's reaction, she switched on the news on the wireless, and was stunned to discover that three of the IRA's most senior men had been snatched from Mountjoy's exercise yard by helicopter, and her husband was one of them. The others were JB O'Hagan and Kevin Mallon.

▲▲▲

Seamus Twomey's father was one of the founders of Fianna Éireann, the IRA's youth organisation, so it was no surprise when his son joined in 1936, at the age of seventeen. A year later, he joined the IRA. He was interned in 1939, when war broke out, and wasn't released until 1946. During those years, he languished on the infamous prison ship, the *Al Rawdah*, until he was transferred to Crumlin Road jail to sit out the remainder of the war. Despite many attempts to escape from both prisons, he was always thwarted and seemed destined never to escape. After his release, he settled down to civilian life as the forties campaign fizzled out. Though he always kept in touch with the movement, he was not involved in the IRA's 1956-62 border campaign. Instead, Twomey settled in Belfast to raise a family, whilst working as a 'runner' in a bookie's shop. But when in 1969 the Troubles started in Belfast, he quickly responded to the call to arms, and reported back for active duty to defend the Divis area along with many of his former comrades from the 1940s. 'The Fighting Forties Club', these veterans were derogatorily called, but despite this derision he proved a resilient volunteer and was instrumental in the establishment of the Provisional IRA (the movement had split early on into two factions, the Provisionals and the Officials). He rose quickly through the ranks of the Provos to become OC of Belfast the following year. His profile was much lower than that of most republicans at the time, and his appearance was not known to many. Just as in Michael Collins's day, this proved a useful asset. Republican legend has it that the British army once raided a house in west Belfast looking for him, but all they found was an old man sitting by the fire. They searched the house and then apologised to the old man for disturbing him. 'No problem,' mumbled Twomey from under his false beard.

The IRA were convinced that it was to be a short war. In the early 1970s, *Republican News* would proclaim each year to be the year of victory. There was now enough momentum behind the movement to make the North ungovernable, to really bring the British to the negotiation table as Collins had done in the 1920s. They felt they had the Brits by the short and curlies. The first step towards this objective was bringing down Stormont after its fifty-year reign, and after it fell on 24 March 1972, the British assumed direct control of the North. Under Twomey, the Belfast brigade continued its bombing campaign until a bilateral truce with the British was negotiated on 26 June, on the understanding that any resumption of hostilities required twenty-four hours' notice. For the first time since the outbreak of the Troubles, Twomey was able to return to his home for a while, but this turned out to be his only period spent there openly until his death in 1989.

As Belfast OC, Twomey had a reputation for being taciturn and uncompromising, but a useful man to have at your shoulder at a negotiation table. He was therefore included in the top-level IRA delegation that flew to England for a secret meeting with Home Secretary William Whitelaw and his officials on 7 July 1972. The Provos were pushing for immediate withdrawal from Irish soil, to be completed by the year 1975, while the British were merely negotiating for an end to the escalating violence. There was little hope of agreement, and some among the British delegation stated afterwards that the Irish delegation were negotiating as if they had fought the British to the brink of surrender and were offering them a dignified escape route. To them, the Irish were simply not being realistic. The IRA delegation read like a 'who's who' of Sinn Féin and IRA personnel, including Seán Mac Stiofáin, Dáithí Ó Conaill, Martin McGuinness, Ivor Bell, Gerry Adams and of course, Twomey, but they came home empty-handed. Twomey couldn't understand why the British went to such drastic lengths to get them over to the negotiations and then offered them nothing. He stated afterwards that all they were

Right: This Wanted poster, offering what was then a substantial amount of money for Gunter Schutz's (alias Hans Marschner) recapture, illustrates the degree to which De Valera's government was anxious to maintain its neutrality during the war.

Below: A young Gunter Schutz embarking on a military career that was to bring him to Ireland as a spy.

Bottom: Gunter with Una Mackey, whom he met at a dance in Athlone towards the end of the war and later married.

COURTESY IRISH MILITARY ARCHIVES

GARDA SIOCHANA

£500 REWARD

The above sum will be paid to any person giving information resulting in the arrest of HANS MARSCHNER, German internee who escaped from custody at Mountjoy *Prison on the night of 15th February, 1942*

30 yrs. of age, 5ft. 9ins., complexion pale, hair dark brown, eyes brown, scar between eyes and on left cheek.   Speaks English well.

Information may be given to any Garda Station.

Proportionate reward will be paid for information con-

COURTESY MICHAEL SCHUTZ

COURTESY MICHAEL SCHUTZ

CHAPTER 2

THE NATIONAL LIBRARY OF IRELAND

Above: The ominous façade of Derry's prison. Only one turret remains today, which is now a loyalist museum. This site is in the Fountain housing estate, the only loyalist enclave in that part of the city, the bogside of the river, a flashpoint during the Troubles.

Below: This photograph of the Derry escapees was taken after their recapture by Free State forces near St Johnston in County Donegal. Their welcome in the Free State was not quite what they had anticipated.

FLUTTERBY FILMS

ASSOCIATED NEWSPAPERS

Above: The gable end of a house in Ballymurphy, west Belfast, depicting the *Maidstone* escapee Jim Bryson (right) with his favourite weapon, the Lewis machine-gun.

Left: Prisoners on the *Maidstone* avail of their exercise period to scrutinise the ship's security, while a British army sentry (below) looks on.

RTE

THE IRISH TIMES

Above: In a typical propaganda coup, the seven escapees resurface in Dublin for a press conference.

Below: Left to right: Tommy Toland, Jim Bryson, Peter Rodgers, Tucker Kane, Tommy Gorman, Martin Taylor, Sean Convery. In this *Reservoir Dogs*-style pose, the seven escapees are paraded before the press. Only four of them are still alive – Bryson, Toland and Kane were killed on active service.

CHAPTER 4

Top right: Captain Thompson Boyes, the hijacked helicopter pilot.

Right middle: Garda forensics investigate the helicopter for fingerprints. The escape was a monumental embarrassment for the new coalition government which vowed to get tough on the Provos.

Left Bottom: The scene of the crime, Mountjoy's D wing exercise yard. The escape was immortalised in the Wolfe Tones' 'Helicopter Song', which shot to Number 1 a week after the event. The song was immediately banned.

Bottom right: Seamus Twomey, Chief of Staff of the IRA, in his trademark dark shades. Not even his chronic vertigo prevented him from escaping in the helicopter.

RTE

RTE

FLUTTERBY FILMS

LARRY DOHERTY

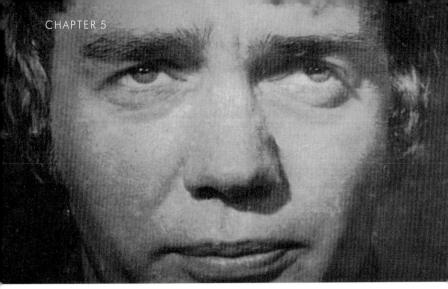

CHAPTER 5

PADRAIG KENNELLY

Above: This is the poster that Kenneth Littlejohn made of himself in order to woo the daughter of millionaire Hans Liebherr in Kerry.

Below: Every new member of the Kerry flying club in Farranfore airport had his tie cut off and suspended over the bar on obtaining his pilot's licence. Kenneth Littlejohn's tie was still hanging in the airport bar when he hit the headlines for his spectacular raid on the AIB in Grafton Street in 1972, the biggest heist in the history of the state at the time.

PADRAIG KENNELLY

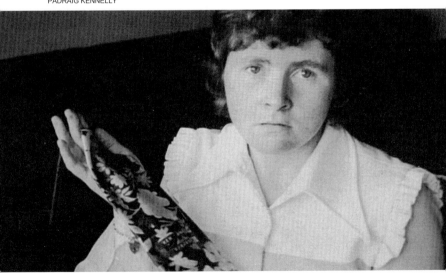

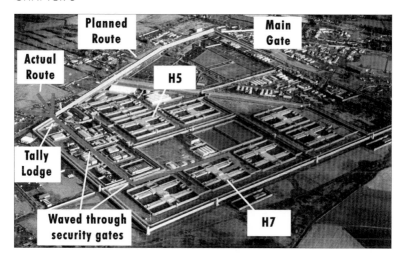

Above: The Maze prison, showing the route of the escape from block H7 through to the Tally Lodge, where plans went awry and the escapees scattered instead of going the full journey to the main entrance gate.

Below: Arrest of two Maze escapees, Hugh Corey and Patrick McIntyre, at a house near Castlewellan. Pictures taken from an RUC video of the arrest.

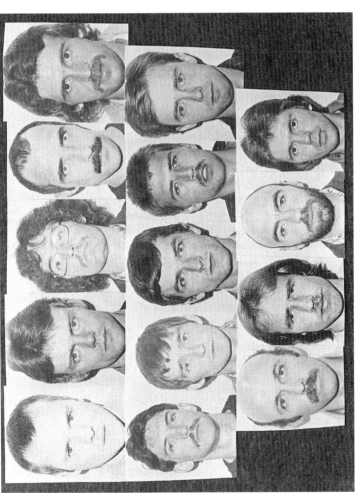

Have you seen these men? The RUC issued this leaflet in an effort to hunt down the Maze fugitives. Only fourteen of the nineteen who actually escaped are pictured here. **Top row** (left to right): Gerard Fryers, Robert Russell, Gerry Kelly, Paul Brennan, Dermot McNally.

Middle row: Seamus Campbell, Padraig McKearney, Dermot Finnucane, Patrick McIntyre, James Smyth.

Bottom Row: Paul Kane, Brendan Mead, Gerard McDonnell, James Clarke.

offered was liquid refreshments, and he knew too much about Irish history to fall for that one. Two days later, the ceasefire ended because of a dispute over the re-housing of Catholics in a loyalist area called Lenadoon, adjacent to Andersonstown. Twomey was trying to negotiate with the British, who had erected a barricade at the mouth of the estate. Crowds of UDA men had formed on one side of the peace line whilst supporters of the Catholic families were gathered on the other, and the situation was tense. When a British Saracen rammed a Catholic family's furniture lorry, Twomey took this to mean that hostilities had recommenced, and he returned to war.

Compromise was no longer on the agenda as each side accused the other of breaking the truce. One of the major campaigns the Belfast brigade embarked on at that time was a series of car bombs on 21 July, later to be known as Bloody Friday. Over twenty car bombs were detonated in under an hour, and the authorities simply couldn't cope with the scale and magnitude of the destruction. Nine people were killed, and dozens more were injured, mostly civilians going about their shopping on a Friday afternoon. It was a PR disaster for the Provos, coming at a time when they were riding high as the defenders of Catholic Belfast. Bloody Friday became a watershed in the IRA's relationship with nationalists, North and South. Just a fortnight after the peace talks, both sides were now entrenched.

Twomey's meteoric rise through the echelons of the IRA leadership brought him to the level of Chief of Staff by the end of 1972, a position he was to hold until his arrest the following September. He was brought before the Special Criminal Court in Dublin charged with membership of the IRA, contrary to Section 21 of the Offences Against the State Act. His only statement in court was, 'I refuse to recognise this British-orientated quisling court.' As he was led away he shouted, 'Up Belfast! Up the Provos!' He was handed down a sentence of five years, but his time in Mountjoy would last a mere three weeks.

▲▲▲

In common with Twomey, the second helicopter escapee, JB O'Hagan, had also been interned during World War II. He got his republican ethos from his mother's side of the family – she had a brother who received the Victoria Cross for bravery from the British army but gave it back and joined the IRA. It was this maternal uncle who inspired the young Joe (as JB was called) to join the IRA when he returned from boarding school at eighteen. In 1942, while he was working in his father's poultry business, he was picked up by the authorities and interned in Belfast's Crumlin Road jail, not emerging until the war ended in 1945. As O'Hagan entered into adulthood, he was deeply religious and a staunch Catholic, and it was as much for his religion, as for his country, that he chose to resist British occupation. When the forties campaign petered out, O'Hagan settled down in Lurgan, married his girlfriend Bernadette, and started a family. But peace didn't last forever and he was again called to fight in December 1956, when the IRA embarked on its border campaign. He went on the run and didn't return home for seven years. He was arrested in the Republic in 1958 and sent to the Curragh internment camp, where he was held for what was his second period of internment, but his first as a guest of a different nation. He soon teamed up with the more militant campaigners amongst the one hundred and eighty-five internees in the camp, and his mind turned to an escape bid.

The IRA camp staff nominated himself and another volunteer, Charlie Murphy, to embark on an escape. However, when word was sent to GHQ, the Chief of Staff, Sean Cronin, decreed that Dáithí Ó Conaill and Ruairí Ó Brádaigh should come out instead, much to the chagrin of Murphy and O'Hagan. On Wednesday, 24 September, the escape plan was executed. Dummies were made up and put into the two escapees' beds, so that the warder's head count would tally. During a game of football in the yard, a blanket was smuggled to a point where spectators stood at the periphery of the surrounding fencing. When the guards' attention was distracted, the blanket was laid down and the other internees kicked loose grass on top of it as camouflage. Ó Conaill and Ó Brádaigh then crawled under it and waited until nightfall. Once the internees had left the yard, it was a security precaution that two prison officers would check the perimeter fencing, to ensure that it was not cut and that nobody was hiding out there. Cunningly, the volunteers left a good quality cap at the point where the two men were hiding, hoping that it would distract the guards from what really lay there. That night, when the internees were anxiously listening for the sound of an alarm, the chief prison officer came in with the fancy cap, asking if it belonged to anyone. They knew then that the boys had succeeded in getting away.

The Curragh camp was surrounded by four armed sentry posts. The internees constantly debated as to whether the 'Free Staters', as the Irish soldiers were called, would open fire if they simply tried to run out of the camp through the barbed wire. The older men were suspicious. They remembered John Kavanagh being shot dead as he tried to tunnel out of Cork jail in August of 1940, and Barney Casey suffering a similar fate trying to escape from the Curragh at the same time. Nothing had changed, in the meantime, to reassure them that attitudes had improved. Younger internees, like JB O'Hagan, were willing to risk it, even though the consequences were potentially deadly. The older generation banned this kind of escape, as the potential loss of life would be too great and they were sure that internment would be short-lived.

The younger internees simply didn't have the patience, and ignored these orders. In the fading winter daylight of 3 December 1958, they struck. They swiftly overpowered the officers in the yard while others cut the surrounding wire, and over thirty of the internees broke out. The army soldiers didn't open fire, but the sergeant on duty used his hand-gun and shot a number of the escapees in the leg. As O'Hagan returned to help free a comrade who had become entangled in the barbed wire, ammonia grenades were cast among the sprawling escapees, and to O'Hagan it felt like the ground came up to hit him in the face. Disabled by the gas, he was easily arrested, but sixteen of the escapees managed to evade capture and nobody had been killed. They had called the State's bluff and it had paid off. Twice in three months, O'Hagan had come tantalisingly close to escaping.

He was released in 1959 by the government in the Republic, as the IRA's campaign was considered in disarray and less of a threat. He returned to active service north of the border, where he was responsible for demolishing the Dungannon Territorial Army barracks with 50lbs of explosives. Whilst on the run, he teamed up with the Curragh blanket escapee Dáithí Ó Conaill. The pair were being escorted, by a young teenager on a bicycle, from one safe house to another in Ardboe in County Tyrone when, as they passed a narrow country gateway, they were ambushed. Parked at the gateway was a laundry van full of B Specials and RUC officers. The first that O'Hagan knew of it was when the van's headlights lit up, and a gun was pushed under his chin. Ó Conaill, who was nearer to the side of the road, tried to run away across a field, but was shot five times and severely wounded. Both men were arrested, and O'Hagan was sent to Crumlin Road jail until his eventual release in September 1963. He again returned to civilian life, but unrest reared its head again as the sixties gave way to the seventies. When the Northern authorities introduced internment once more, O'Hagan, now shy from having been interned in the previous two campaigns, went on the run as an active republican. In May 1973, O'Hagan and Seamus Twomey were attending the funeral of a fallen comrade in Cavan town when, as the cortège passed through Bailinagh, the Gardaí swooped. Twomey managed to slip their grasp, but they picked up O'Hagan and charged him with membership of the IRA. He was sentenced to twelve months for membership and dispatched to Mountjoy. Also lifted in this swoop was the third helicopter escapee, Kevin Mallon.

▲▲▲

On 17 August 1957, RUC Sergeant Arthur Ovens, a father of three, was sent to search a small derelict cottage near Coalis-land in County Tyrone. He approached with caution, suspecting it to be a hideout. He gave the front door a powerful

BREAK-OUT!

kick below the latch, and as it burst open he was engulfed by an explosion. In the aftermath, a major round-up was ordered to track down those responsible for his murder, and the prime suspects were two local twenty-one-year-olds, Kevin Mallon and Patrick Talbot, who were arrested. It was felt that they would be executed if found guilty, and under these circumstances, the policy of not recognising the court was abandoned and a prominent Welsh barrister, Elwyn Jones, was hired to defend the pair. Mallon and Talbot alleged that they were subjected to torture during interrogation, carried out by officers furious at the loss of a colleague. The pair were acquitted on the murder charge when evidence of ill-treatment was produced, but Mallon was sentenced to fourteen years for arms and conspiracy offences. He spent the next few years in Belfast's Crumlin Road jail, but was released in 1963 after the border campaign had come to an end. One of two things occurs in these circumstances: you can take your hiding, get on with your life after your release, and put the incident behind you, or you can give it back with interest. As he rose in the ranks of the IRA, Mallon proved to be a powerful adversary.

▲▲▲

By mid-1973, internment in the North was taking its toll, and in the South the new coalition government, led by Liam Cosgrave of Fine Gael, was strangling the movement. It had come to power on the law-and-order ticket, with a stated policy of 'getting tough on crime'. The government needed to curb the activities of the IRA, who were becoming dangerously powerful as their ranks swelled as a result of the Troubles. The government had significant powers at its command in their fight against republicans. Section 31 of the Broadcasting Act censored proscribed terrorist organisations and cut off their access to the airwaves. The Special Criminal Court was achieving convictions at a tremendous rate with non-jury courts. It was under this government that the notorious Garda 'heavy gang' began to operate, and they got very tough on the Provos. Arrests and convictions followed. The Provos were also their own worst enemy, however. Although there was no internment in the Republic at the time, the IRA's policy of not recognising the courts left them open to what was effectively internment in all but name. Many Provos were rounded up and accused of membership by a superintendent in the Gardaí; the court case was a *fait accompli* as there would be no defence, merely a statement of non-recognition, and membership carried a mandatory twelve-month sentence. By October of 1973, the command structure of the IRA was seriously curbed, with three of their top men, their former Chief of Staff, Seamus Twomey, JB O'Hagan and Kevin Mallon, all languishing in the same Dublin jail.

The government tried to introduce a limited form of criminalisation for the IRA prisoners in Mountjoy. At this time both sections of the IRA, the Officials and the Provisionals, enjoyed segregation and the wearing of their own clothes. They also ran the wings through their command structure. However, the new regime tried to introduce prison uniforms and abolish the republicans' segregation. The last thing the Provos needed, especially with their escape plans gaining momentum, was ODCs (ordinary decent criminals) in their midst, who would readily divulge information to the warders

BREAK-OUT!

in return for a few fags a week. They needed their own space with no interference, so there was no alternative for the prisoners but to embark on the time-honoured practice of the hunger strike. This weapon had been in the Celtic armoury since before medieval times, when a wronged subject would starve himself on the king's threshold to embarrass him into restitution. Eight prisoners in all refused food, and one of them was JB O'Hagan. The strike afforded the Provos a greater hand in dealing with the governor, as his decisions and actions would be held under a media spotlight. After twenty-one days, the authorities relented and the prisoners were able to return to the regime to which they had become accustomed. They could now plot and plan their escapes unhindered.

A small clique, comprising only five volunteers, was established in the jail as an escape committee. Senior prisoners and veterans of previous prison regimes, such as Joe Cahill and Éamonn Mac Thomáis, were always consulted. The committee was made aware of a trapdoor on the top floor of the wing, which led on to the roof. With a little work, they could break through the roof tiles and use sheets to clamber down the wall into the yard. Word was sent in that an attempt would be made to spring the three senior republicans, Twomey, O'Hagan and Mallon. The first attempt at a break-out was a straightforward affair. Explosives were smuggled in; the escapees were to use them to blow a hole through a door inside the prison and make their way into the exercise yard, where there would be a rope ladder waiting to enable them to get over the exterior wall.

The GHQ of the IRA asked the Dublin brigade to provide the requisite getaway services. A team of young Dublin volunteers was assigned to take over a house on Glengariff Parade, which ran adjacent to the eastern end of the prison, and to have a getaway car on standby. At 9.00am on the chosen day, they had taken over the house and lay in wait in the backyard, at the end of which was Mountjoy's enormous perimeter wall. They were poised to cast a rope ladder over the wall to facilitate the escape. Although they were armed with real guns, no bullets were issued to them: Order No. 8 from the army council was that no Gardaí were to be shot in the operation. If it became necessary, the volunteers were to sacrifice themselves to facilitate the escape of any of the men. Such were their orders. They cast the rope ladder over the wall and waited anxiously for the men to arrive. After some time, it became evident that the plan had gone astray on the inside. The escapees failed to gain access to the yard and the rope ladder had been spotted. A combination of Gardaí and prison officers descended on the house, but the volunteers made good their escape. For the IRA, it was back to the drawing board.

▲▲▲

One particular volunteer on the outside had been busy at that drawing board. He was watching television one Sunday afternoon when he saw a movie featuring a daring helicopter prison escape. Why not? he thought. It could be over in minutes. The idea was pitched to GHQ staff and a meeting was held in Dublin's RDS to discuss possibilities. The idea of a helicopter escape was not a new one, but because it could be used only once, it had been kept in the back pocket as a trump card. It's understood to have first been mooted in Long Kesh internment camp as a means of getting Gerry Adams out, but was ruled out for military reasons: the Kesh was near a British army base, where faster and more sophisticated helicopters, that could easily catch a hired civilian chopper, were readily available. The idea had also been suggested to spring another prisoner, held in the UK, but here the support structure would not be as easily obtainable on the ground. It was considered a wasteful deployment of what was really a one-off escape weapon. Ultimately GHQ approved the escape idea and the plan was set in motion.

The manager of Irish Helicopters opened the offices in the Westpoint hangar in Dublin airport on 20 October 1973, a crisp autumn morning. Beside him hung a cheeky advertisement for the company: 'Going somewhere in a hurry? People using helicopters include: Chief executives, jockeys, photographers, spies, gamblers, golfers, smugglers, clergymen, ambassadors, and foreign industrialists.' He was accustomed to foreigners hiring their services, so it was no surprise when a slim, well-groomed, bespectacled American, calling himself Mr Leonard, arrived at the depot wishing to hire a helicopter. The manager listened with amusement to his outrageously over-the-top American accent as he produced a large Ordnance Survey map of County Laois, on which he circled different locations and described what was needed. He required a large chopper for himself and his American companions, for an aerial photographic shoot above the rock of Dunmace in County Laois, and it needed to be big enough to carry all his photographic equipment as well as the driver.

In the hangar he was shown the company's fleet, and he chose the French-made five-seater *Alouette 2* helicopter as being the one for the job. He booked the helicopter for 31 October, at a cost of IR£80 per hour of flying time, and was strangely insistent that Irish Helicopters take a deposit for the booking, even when the manager assured him that this was not necessary. They never asked for booking deposits, yet the American seemed to be trying to force the money on him. That may be the way things are done in the States, the manager thought, and the visitor was assured that the chopper would be ready on the appointed day and at the appointed time. Satisfied with this, Mr Leonard headed for the exit. As he left the building, the manager noticed the visitor's shoes for the first time: they were dirty, and strangely out of keeping with his impeccably groomed suit. The shoes maketh the man, he thought to himself. The booking was made in the name of Mr Leonard, c/o the Royal Dublin hotel.

Security at the helicopter depot appeared to be quite lax, and thus the first part of the operation was set in motion. The remainder required co-ordination. The helicopter was to be hijacked by a volunteer in Laois, then landed in the yard during the prisoners' exercise period. It was then to be flown to Baldoyle racecourse, where a getaway car would be waiting. A group of Dublin volunteers, who had been involved in the bungled escape over the wall, were drafted in to steal a car in the city and drive it to a pre-arranged spot near the racecourse. They were to pick up the passengers and bring them to a safe house, from where they would be dispersed to accommodation around the city. Rock-solid safe

BREAK-OUT!

houses were put on standby. These were no ordinary escapees, but three of the Provos' top men.

On the inside, the operation had to be kept as secret as possible; in the run-up to the escape, only a half a dozen volunteers were informed of the impending flight. But restraining the prison officers required more bodies than that. The more prisoners that were in the yard on the day, the easier it was for them to outmanoeuvre the warders, and so a deliberately intense football match was arranged, to ensure maximum interest and participation by the prisoners. Kevin Mallon was selected to semaphore the landing helicopter with white pieces of cloth, while others were assigned the job of restraining the officers who were always stationed in pairs at the entrance to the yard and in each of its four corners. The plan was flawless. There's going to be some fireworks on Halloween night, the planners thought.

On 31 October, the manager of Irish Helicopters looked at the hire schedule for the day. That American eejit Leonard was due to take a helicopter for a photographic shoot. As the morning progressed towards lunchtime, he figured that this guy wasn't going to turn up because the weather had taken a turn for the worse; it wasn't a good day for aerial photography. As a result, he took his time over his lunch and arrived late back at the depot. Leonard was there waiting for him, dancing a jig with impatience. You'd swear he had a connecting flight. 'Where's your camera gear?' the manager asked him, but Leonard said that he was going to pick it up in Stradbally. The manager introduced Leonard to his pilot for the day, Captain Thompson Boyes, and they talked briefly about Leonard's requirements. His priority was to get moving. He gave Boyes the co-ordinates of the field in Strad-bally where he was to land to pick up his photographic equipment, and where he would also take the doors off the chopper in order to facilitate unobstructed filming.

As a result of Leonard's late departure, the operation had fallen behind schedule. Down in D wing's exercise yard in Mountjoy, Mallon, Twomey and O'Hagan gazed skywards, where all the clouds seemed to merge into one big grey blanket. The soccer game intensified underneath, and every time the ball was kicked in the air, their eyes didn't follow it downwards. There were eight prison officers in the yard. One of them watched the three IRA leaders and, looking at the ex-Chief of Staff, Twomey, noticed that he was wearing leather shoes. That's strange, the man thought to himself, he never wears shoes. Twomey was a great man for the Moses sandals; hail, rain or shine, he always wore Moses sandals to the prison yard. At that moment, the football bounced towards him; he kicked it back to the prisoners, and his mind drifted off to other matters.

▲▲▲

In Dublin's city centre, the three young IRA volunteers set about stealing a getaway car. They were told how important this escape bid was, and failure in this part of the operation would have dire consequences. They walked down Eden Quay, alongside the river, and tried a number of cars that were parked there. Inexperienced car thieves, they were unable to get any of them started. Time was running short, and none of them wanted to suffer the consequences of arriving late to the pickup point at the disused Baldoyle racecourse. As they became increasingly frustrated, and were running out of time, they decided to hire, and then hijack, a taxi.

En route to Stradbally, Captain Boyes was eager to impress his American guest as he had only started working for Irish Helicopters the previous week. He landed in a field near Stradbally, which belonged to bachelor farmer Tommy Kelly, and as he was watching his gauges a gun was put to his head by a masked man. Leonard then disappeared, and the gunman climbed aboard brandishing a rifle and a pistol. Boyes was ordered to follow instructions and he would not be harmed. He was also told, in no uncertain terms, that if he fouled up this operation he would get a bullet through the head. Boyes, a Protestant, had grown up in Newtownards, County Down, and knew immediately that this was an IRA operation. He also knew that they did not make empty threats. Without telling the pilot what his mission was, the armed volunteer ordered him to follow the Royal canal into Dublin. He obeyed, scared out of his wits.

Across the city, another driver was scared out of his wits. At 2.30pm, a taxi driver, operating from the rank in O'Connell Street, picked up three nice-looking kids, a girl and two lads, who were going to Malahide. Halfway there, one of them pulled a whopping Colt .45 on him. This was no ordinary weapon. This was a Dirty Harry job. The kid spoke in a measured tone: 'We're not criminals, we're not going to rob you. We just need your car for an hour or two and you will be fully paid your hire fee and the car will be returned to you.' The size of the weapon didn't reassure him. The volunteers didn't quite know what to do with him, as they were supposed to have stolen their own car. If they held on to him he would just be a burden, but if they dumped him somewhere, he could raise the alarm and jeopardise the operation, so he was locked up, bound and gagged, in a safe location.

▲▲▲

As they approached Dublin city, Boyes was informed about the mission to lift three men from Mountjoy jail. He was concerned on two fronts. He explained to the hijacker that helicopters sometimes couldn't take off in enclosed spaces. If the jail's walls were too close, there wouldn't be enough upswing for the chopper to lift off the ground. Of greater concern to him was the weight of the chopper. They had a full tank of fuel, as he had not planned on four passengers, and it was extremely risky to try and lift this weight. They might get so far and then fall like a brick. The volunteer was unperturbed, and simply ordered him to follow instructions.

It was now 3.35pm and O'Hagan had started to pace up and down. The football match had lost its edge, and many of the prisoners had returned inside. Some of them were asked to stay behind, and told with a wink and a nod that 'something was going to happen.' This air of mystery kept most of them interested, and they started to circle the yard. Dusk was falling and the temperature was dropping. By this stage, there were only twenty-three left outside. The agreed plan was that, if for some reason the escape could not be achieved that day, it would be postponed for twenty-four hours. It was looking more and more likely that this would be the case, when suddenly the unmistakable sound of a helicopter began to reverberate around the yard.

The volunteers sprang into action, but then stalled as the chopper flew over the yard and swung away. Was the landing site too narrow, leaving the rotary blades too wide for the perimeter walls? All these questions were quickly answered when the helicopter swung low into the canal end of the yard. Galvanised into action, the prisoners moved on the warders. They circled the eight prison officers and scuffles started amid the confusion. One of the officers lifted a breeze block to throw at the rear blade of the chopper, which would have prevented its flight, but was quickly overpowered. It was impossible for the officers to prevent the escape. Aside from the prisoners impeding them, they could hardly see in front of them as the chopper blades were stirring up all the dust and debris that littered the enclosed yard. Kevin Mallon, semaphoring with two white rags, directed the pilot to the ground whilst keeping in mind the distance between the rotary blades and the perimeter walls. Mallon was the youngest and fittest, and was first into the chopper, with O'Hagan following and Twomey bringing up the rear.

Overcome by the excitement, one of the IRA volunteers thought he would seize this opportunity to escape and he grabbed onto the rising chopper. According to Boyes, they were already over their maximum weight and another passenger would definitely drag them down. The unofficial escapee was firmly told to stay put. The chopper began its unimpeded rise skywards, but Twomey hadn't quite boarded properly, and was half in and half out. The door was not closed correctly behind him, and O'Hagan was doing his utmost to keep him from falling out. He had one arm around Twomey, to hold him in the aircraft, while his other hand held a gun, and as he didn't have a free arm he couldn't close the door. In a flash, he handed Mallon the pistol, lunged forward, and managed to pull the door closed with all three safely inside. The helicopter rose slowly, rocking from side to side as it tried to counteract the turbulence rebounding from the surrounding walls. Eventually, it ascended over the prison wall. Up, up and away!

It was only then, with this minor panic over, that O'Hagan was able to savour the moment and look down to the yard below, sinking away from them. He could make out the prisoners screaming and dancing with delight. It was a gleeful sight. In contrast, the prison officers were rooted to the spot in disbelief. In a mixture of rage and confusion, one of the officers ordered: 'Close the gates, close the fucking gates!' It was not, perhaps, a particularly appropriate measure.

▲▲▲

The three volunteers had taken the taxi plate off their car, and sped towards the pre-allocated rendezvous. As arranged, they parked beside a brightly coloured house near the racecourse, which would easily be spotted from the air. They sat there waiting, edgy. No sign. The driver looked across the road, where a motorbike Garda had just pulled up and was looking suspiciously in their direction. They knew they looked dubious, but were at a loss for what to do. Inspired, the driver lifted the bonnet and started to examine the engine, as if the car had broken down. The Garda still looked on. There was no shifting this bloke. There was nothing for it only to leave the spot, do a circle, and hope that the Garda had disappeared by the time they returned.

Capt. Thompson Boyes raised the chopper above Dublin and angled towards Baldoyle racecourse, as instructed. What was he to do? He had seen all their faces by now. Were they going to waste him once his usefulness had passed? Would he get that promised bullet through the head? He wouldn't be the first, nor would he be the last. He thought of crash-landing, driving the chopper into a building and taking them all with him. A kamikaze mission. He looked around briefly, and his eyes met those of one of the men he had plucked from the yard. He recognised him. Maybe he could plead with him. Would he remember me? The prisoner he recognised was JB O'Hagan. Boyes had seen him before in a different yard, not a prison yard but a farmyard. When he was a child, O'Hagan used to come around to their farm, collect the old hens that were finished laying eggs, and sell them on. Was it for dog food?

His mind was processing these thoughts at lightning speed when one of the men reassured him that he would come to no harm. He was also told that he would be paid for his services. Two of the three prisoners were in jubilant mood, looking down at the ant-like people below, knowing that even if they were to be caught now, they had pulled off a daring escape. The other was Seamus Twomey. To him, this helicopter ride was a nightmare; he simply buried his head in his hands and prayed for it to end. All his life he had suffered from chronic vertigo; he couldn't even sit in the upper Cusack Stand in Croke Park, and this airborne trip was like torture. Though to him it seemed like an eternity, they touched down in Baldoyle after a mere six minutes. They thanked their pilot, told him, 'We'll sort you out for that,' and left him there, ashen-faced but grateful to be alive after his ordeal. The three escapees and the IRA volunteer looked around for their getaway car. It wasn't there.

Having done a quick circle, the hijacked taxi returned to the brightly coloured house. As the volunteers crested the brow of a hill, they noticed with relief that the cop had gone, but to their horror the chopper had already landed, and they hadn't been there to meet it. Shit, now they were in real trouble! By the time they got to the spot, the escapees were in the process of hijacking another car. Earlier on, the volunteers hadn't managed to steal a car with a full half-hour to spare, but these pros had hijacked one in seconds and were in the process of getting in. The hijacked taxi sped alongside them and when the doors opened, the escapees abandoned the car they were in the process of commandeering and jumped into the taxi, which zoomed off. The volunteers later abandoned the vehicle in Portmarnock's Carrick Hill Road, by which time all three escapees were securely billeted in safe houses on Dublin's northside. The taxi driver received his fare the following week. He didn't argue about the price.

It was a major source of embarrassment for the new government who, in opposition, had accused the Fianna Fáil government of being ambivalent towards the Provos. The unfortunate Minister for Justice, Paddy Cooney, was on a visit to Turkey at the time of the escape, and the opposition got great mileage from this. In the Dáil they quipped that you could forgive the prison officers for mistakenly thinking the helicopter to be a visit from the minister, as he spent all his time in the air. The Taoiseach, Liam Cosgrave, raged that there would be 'no hiding place' for the escapees. A huge dragnet was ordered to hunt down these dangerous terrorists in a manhunt involved some twenty thousand security personnel. There were rumours circulating that the three had been smuggled to the UK on a trawler from Howth, but in actual fact they were much closer to home. That night, as the news broke in Belfast, republicans piled their Halloween bonfires higher and higher in honour of the exhilarating escape.

The ultimate consequence of the escape was the movement of all politicos to the maximum-security prison at Portlaoise. Ten days after the escape, at six in the morning, all the republican prisoners in both Mountjoy and the Curragh were taken there in a convoy. The government did not want egg on its face again, so armed soldiers were deployed to guard the perimeter of the prison and intersecting wires were erected over the yard, to prevent a repeat of the mechanical bird's escape.

Republican troubadours started scribbling immediately, and the Wolfe Tones had a smash hit with their 'Helicopter Song'. Based on the exploits of that Halloween night, it was immediately banned, copper-fastening its success as it sold twelve thousand copies in a single week and crashed in at number one in the Irish charts. The cartoonists relished the government's embarrassment, and this 'spectacular' grabbed headlines throughout the world.

▲▲▲

The helicopter break-out inspired copycat escapes internationally. One of the most violent of these occurred early on the morning of 18 June 1990, when a helicopter approached Kent maximum-security institution in Canada and hovered over the industrial area inside the perimeter fence. The craft attempted to land, but was forced to remain airborne by the approach of a motor patrol vehicle driven by armed prison guards. Gunshots were fired from the helicopter at the patrol vehicle, and one struck a correctional officer in the leg, seriously wounding him. Officers in the patrol vehicle returned fire, and during this exchange the helicopter descended low enough for two prisoners, Robert Ford and David Thomas, to jump aboard and make good their escape.

In Chile, in December of 1996, a faction of the Manuel Rodríguez Patriotic Front (FPMR) executed the shocking helicopter escape of four of its leaders from a maximum-security prison near Santiago. The four men leapt into a basket lowered by the helicopter, whilst startled prison officers took shelter from the spray of gunfire coming from above. Suspecting IRA involvement, members of Chile's Carabineros police force came to Ireland, in March 1997, to seek help with their investigations. They alleged that two republican sisters from County Clare, Christine and Frances Shannon, had posed as tourists and rented the helicopter; but efforts to extradite the sisters were rejected by the Irish courts. Other copycat escapes occurred in Brazil in January of 2002, and twice from the same French prison in March of 2001 and April of 2003, putting an end to the theory that it was a method that could work only once. Two bungled copycat escapes occurred in the USA in 1989 and 2000; in both instances, the helicopters crashed shortly after leaving the prison and the fleeing prisoners were recaptured. The IRA, who prided themselves as pioneers in guerrilla warfare, could now put the helicopter escape down as a new development in revolutionary war. An active service unit within the IRA was also to be inspired by such a daring exploit. Early in 1974, they seized a helicopter and forced the pilot, at gunpoint, to fly across the border. The objective this time was not a daring jailbreak, but to drop two milk churns, packed with explosives, into Strabane's RUC station. Luckily for the station's occupants, neither of the lethal churns detonated.

▲▲▲

Twomey was no longer Chief of Staff after his escape, but he remained on the army council as an active republican. He was eventually to resurface, on 2 December 1977, in the leafy suburb of Sandycove in south Dublin. The Special Branch had been tipped off by Belgian police about a concealed arms shipment, which was to be delivered to a bogus company with an address in this part the city. In an attempt to arrest those behind the front, the Special Branch swooped on a house in Martello Terrace to discover Twomey outside in his car, wearing his trademark dark shades. Simultaneously, he spotted them. If he could escape their grasp by helicopter, surely he had a fighting chance in a car. After a frenetic high-speed pursuit through the city, he was recaptured in the centre of Dublin. On him, the Branch found documentation about the re-organisation of the IRA along cellular lines, as well as a manual on interrogation-resistance techniques. His arrest was considered by some to be a watershed in the movement, as the leadership of the IRA was then assumed by the next generation of volunteers, who espoused the 'long war' strategy.

Twomey was duly sentenced to finish the remainder of his original sentence, and spent over four years in Portlaoise prison until his eventual release in 1982. He took a less active role in the movement throughout the eighties, as his health was failing, and he died in 1989 in his one-bedroomed apartment in Dublin's Ballybaugh, close to his spiritual home of Croke Park.

O'Hagan was recaptured on Mobhi Road in Dublin, fifteen months after his escape, and was made to complete the remainder of his twelve-month sentence in Portlaoise. After that sentence was finished, he was again arrested, this time in his cell, and sentenced to two more years for escaping. On his release he resumed republican activity, whilst living in exile in County Monaghan, until the peace process enabled him to return to his beloved Lurgan in 1995, where he died on 23 April 2001.

While most escapees immediately go into hiding, or on the run, Kevin Mallon lived quite openly after his escape, almost taunting the authorities. He spent just over a month at liberty, until he was re-captured at a GAA dance in the choicest of locations, the Montague hotel near Portlaoise, on 10 December 1973. It was not long before he found himself on the other side of the town in the maximum-security prison. To Mallon, however, there was no such adjective as escape-proof, and buoyed by his helicopter escapade, he immediately investigated a means of getting out of the jail that prisoners called 'The Bog'. It was with good reason that the Provos were now housed here. In contrast to Mountjoy, which was riddled with escape opportunities, Portlaoise was isolated and visible from a good distance away. It didn't afford the escapee the same opportunities for disappearing into the crowds.

BREAK-OUT!

Once the Provos arrived in Portlaoise, the first item on the agenda was the nomination of escape-committee members. Ideas were bandied about and it wasn't long until a feasible idea was submitted. An Achilles' heel in the security system was identified in the prison's laundry. The laundry was always closed on a Sunday, but one prisoner, who had a reputation for obsessive cleanliness, asked one of the warders if he could gain access as he had left his shirt in there. Whilst left to his own devices, this volunteer snooped around and discovered a potential escape route. There was an exterior stairway from the laundry to the courtyard below. For the prisoners it was a simple matter of smuggling explosives into the prison, and using them to blast their way to the courtyard, from where they would blast their way through an exterior gate.

Explosives were duly smuggled in, and a lazy Sunday afternoon was chosen as the time to strike. The prison would be staffed by a skeleton crew, and those on duty would be taking their lunch break. In the lead-up to the escape, the prisoners amassed all the blue and white shirts they could find and busied themselves with making mock prison uniforms. The plan was to confuse the armed sentry posts, so that they would not be able to distinguish genuine prison officers from escapees in disguise. This would stop them from opening fire. A vanguard team of six escapees was selected, to be followed by a second team of six. Needless to say, Mallon was in the vanguard. After these initial twelve it was a free-for-all, every man for himself.

At 12.30pm on Sunday, 18 August 1974, Liam Brown asked an obliging warder if he could retrieve his jersey, which he had left in the laundry. When he was admitted, the vanguard rushed the door, the guard was relieved of his keys, and the prisoners made their way down the stairwell and blew their way into the courtyard. Close on their heels were the second group, followed by over twenty other republican prisoners. Shock and awe were the key elements. It all had to happen in a flash, before the security forces could act in a co-ordinated manner. The vanguard made their way across the yard and placed the explosives at the perimeter door. With an almighty boom, the door was blown apart. The soldiers fired warning shots over the heads of the rearguard and many of them dropped to the ground and surrendered. One unfortunate escapee was caught up in the enthusiastic tidal wave of prisoners, and found himself outside the prison a mere four days before he was scheduled for release. Doubt-less, he wished he could escape back in instead of having to face the inevitable escape charge. When the authorities man-aged to return the uncooperative prisoners to their cells, they were able to do a headcount and established that a massive nineteen had managed to get away unhindered, among them the man with the indomitable will to be free, Kevin Mallon. A key figure in two of the most spectacular escapes in the his-tory of the twenty-six counties, which occurred within ten months of each other, Mallon, the only survivor of the famous helicopter escape, now lives in north Dublin, where he works as a draughtsman and trains greyhounds. Doubt-less, he could easily beat some of them out of the traps.

It was a measure of the three men's importance within the movement that when Twomey, Mallon and O'Hagan came together again at the end of 1974, it was for peace talks with a group of senior Protestant clerics. The three men were representing the views of the IRA. There were eight republicans in all present at the meeting, not all of them with 'wanted' tags on their heads. The eight clergymen, led by the Reverend William Arlow, included representatives of the Church of Ireland, the Presbyterian Church and the Methodist Church, along with other umbrella Church groups from both England and Ireland. They were determined to enter into meaningful dialogue with the IRA. The meeting was arranged on 20 December 1974 in Smyth's hotel in the sleepy east Clare town of Feakle, a county noted for its strong republican sympathies. Despite this, there was a mole at work and the Special Branch got word that the three men, who had made them a laughing-stock with their helicopter escape, were assembled like sitting ducks in the hotel. Capturing the three in one fell swoop would garner as much publicity as the original escape. They marched into the hotel carrying sub-machine guns, and encountered the president of Sinn Féin, Ruairí Ó Brádaigh, going over notes of their meeting in the lobby. 'Where are the others?' one of the Branchmen inquired. 'Upstairs,' replied Ó Brádaigh, nonchalantly. The armed Branchmen burst into the meeting room, only to find eight rather surprised Protestant clergymen reviewing their notes. The IRA had their own spy in the Branch, warning them of the impending raid, and the three had flown, yet again.

Brothers in Arms

BEFORE GOING TO SLEEP, Kenneth Littlejohn gazed hard at his own reflection in the bathroom mirror. He was trying to out-stare himself. Draped over his naked shoulder was a holster, in which sat a long-barrelled Luger pistol. Without taking his eyes from his own eyes in the mirror, he drew his gun in a flicker. He was quick. He was damn quick. He even took his reflection by surprise sometimes. In the bedroom, his wife, Christine, lay sleeping. He was making some last-minute preparations for his big day. Tomorrow would not dawn just like any other day. Tomorrow he would knock a bank over, the AIB Bank in Dublin's Grafton Street. He pulled the pistol around and pointed it directly between the eyes of his reflection. He was psyched up, he was ready.

The year is 1972. The place is Clogher Head in County Louth. Kenneth and Keith Littlejohn, brothers and *agents provocateurs*, had chosen this sleepy coastal town as their base away from home – its location, just south of the border with Northern Ireland, was the ideal launching pad for forays across the border. Its caravan site was a temporary home to many a republican activist on the run, and in cross-border terms, this was Ireland's El Paso. The introduction of internment in the North had sent these birds of prey flocking south of the border to nest awhile. What better place than this bandit country to infiltrate the IRA as double agents? Even if he was to say so himself, Kenneth was a dab hand at the ould robberies and this was surely to endear him to cash-strapped republican organisations. He considered himself a crucial cog in Britain's counter-insurgence machine in Ireland, and nothing would deter his spying activity for the glorious empire. Fearless, he had unflinchingly mixed with the enemy, and was going to rise to the top of these organisations and topple them from within. Like many a true patriot, if there was personal financial gain into the bargain, he considered it merely a perk of the job.

▲▲▲

These heady days, on Her Majesty's secret service, were in stark contrast to his early career working for the Crown. His first job for the empire was as a lance corporal in the parachute regiment, but he was discharged for stealing a cash box. Kenneth's life of thieving continued when, in 1965, he robbed wages from the firm of Fisher and Ludlow in Birmingham. He was soon arrested and served three years in prison. At the trial, Judge Ashworth described the robbery as 'professional in its execution'. To Kenneth, this was a vote of approval and he tried to adopt this approach in all his future endeavours. On his release, it was time to get back on the straight and narrow as he had a wife, Christine, and his two kids to support, so he capitalised on his penchant for fast cars and set up a car dealership, which kept him afloat for some time.

However, the authorities knew that the draw of the fast

buck was equally attractive to Kenneth and, when a robbery took place at the Midland Motor Cylinder Company in Smethwick on 28 August 1970, it was immediately suspected that he had reverted to his old ways. Kenneth's brother-in-law, Brian Anthony Perks, who worked there as a wages clerk, was found bound and gagged at the rifled safe and charged with complicity in the robbery. With a warrant out for his arrest, Kenneth went on the run. It became imperative to leave the jurisdiction as the police were raiding the homes of friends and associates. The *West Midlands Gazette* issued the following description of Kenneth Brian Littlejohn:

> *Born 19/10/40, 6ft 1in, deeply suntanned, blue eyes, fair hair, long nose, well-built, mastoid scar behind each ear, smart appearance. May have his hair dyed black or be wearing a dark wig. May use the following aliases: Kenneth Austen, Charles Edgar Duverne. Information is to hand that LITTLEJOHN will attempt to leave the country during the August Bank Holiday Period. He is in possession of the stolen money in a canvas holdall and may travel to the continent either as a day tripper without a passport or using a recently obtained passport under an assumed name.*

In fact, Kenneth Austen (a pseudonym Littlejohn used frequently) chose Ireland as the location for his 'new' new beginning and chose the rag trade as his 'new' new line of business. A twenty-nine-year-old heart-throb, he drove into the close-knit rural town of Cahirciveen, in County Kerry, flanked by a German masseuse and a secretary from Dublin, for a Chamber of Commerce meeting. He pulled up in a spanking red MGB sports car, wearing an expensive watch and armed with the business details of his company, Whizz Kids (Ireland) Ltd, which claimed to be Britain's fastest-emerging clothing manufacturer, specialising in ladies' leather hot pants. Its directors were one Kenneth Austen, property tycoon, and his associate Robert Stockman. He was warmly received as a business tycoon by the committee and was asked to make a speech, which he waffled through with some success. He felt almost messianic as the local dignitaries hung on his every word, and lapped up his promises about the economic benefits to their town that the modern clothing industry would bring.

Gaeltarra Éireann, the industrial development association, met with Kenneth and initially encouraged him in his endeavours, as unemployment was rife in this corner of south-west Kerry. With great aplomb, Whizz Kids staged a major publicity venture involving the displaying of his hot-pants products on the tarmac of Kerry's Farranfore airport. Fêted and indulged by the business community of Kerry, he was offered low-rent accommodation and premises. His wife and children came over to stay with him, in a bungalow provided by the people of Cahirciveen, and he relaxed into possibly the most settled period of his life. This domestic bliss was short-lived however, as his head was swiftly turned by the daughter of a multi-millionaire German industrialist, Hans Liebherr, and there was no room in this new romance for a wife and kids. When her family got wind of her new liaison the girl was promptly ordered back to Germany, but Kenneth managed to intercept her at Cork airport and they flew off into a new dawn together. He was smitten by this German heiress and the promise of a comfortable life, but, as with most things in his life, it was not to be.

When he visited Düsseldorf, he noticed she had a large poster of Che Guevara taking pride of place on her bedroom wall. He badly wanted to woo this beauty, and so when he returned to Kerry he got in touch with one of the members of the flying club, a photographer named Padraig Kennelly. He asked Kennelly to take his photograph, emblazon the name Austen beside it in the style of a poster, and he would send it to his sweetheart, who hopefully would replace Che's visage with his own. Blinded in this cloud of love, he even returned to England to ask his wife Christine for a divorce. She refused, and that was the end of that!

He returned to Farranfore with his tail between his legs. People were beginning to wonder when this promised business would be opening, and Kenneth postponed the inevitable by being particularly choosy about the location of his new factory, living off the goodwill of others as long as possible. He bought copious drinks for all and sundry in local pubs, and to copperfasten his reputation as a high flyer (literally) he also took flying lessons at Farranfore airport and graduated with a pilot's licence. The custom in the flying club was that a rookie pilot's tie was cut off with a scissors and suspended over the bar. As the latest graduate, Kenneth's tie had pride of place, and he developed an insatiable appetite for flying. As he soared above the clouds, he imagined himself to be James Bond, ducking and dodging enemy fire, only to return to earth and have to face the tedious reality of his formica-decorated offices in Farranfore airport.

In an attempt to kick-start his enterprise, he ordered a large consignment of hot pants from one manufacturer, Paul Wenzel, but when the time came to cash Kenneth's cheque, it bounced like a rubber ball. Though on the surface, this guy appeared to have the credentials, gently probing questions proved that he knew very little about the rag trade and Gaeltarra were now subtly discouraging him. The charade was gradually wearing thin for his Kerry hosts and now that it was becoming obvious that his promised development was failing to materialise, Kenneth Littlejohn high-tailed it out of Kerry, leaving behind an angry development committee, numerous debts and a string of girlfriends. This high flyer had crash-landed. All he left them, in return for his extravagance, was an empty office in which some items of ladies' clothing were strewn about. While it lasted he had enjoyed the high life of a phony businessman, and the role-playing game of infiltrating a society, pretending to be somebody else, and duping people into believing his tall tales. If only this could be a career! Then again, maybe it could be...

In 1971, his brother-in-law successfully appealed his conviction for the Smethwick robbery and the sentence was quashed. At this point, the 'wanted' tag was taken from Kenneth's head, and replaced by a 'desire to interview'. He could now safely return to London and team up with his younger brother Keith, who had the utmost admiration for his older brother. They had shared some great times, and especially loved to watch Bond movies together. Ever since they were kids, his older brother looked out for him in school and he always had a protective arm around his shoulder. Keith was more introverted than his flamboyant older brother but, admiring his style and bravado, it was not long before he followed in Kenneth's footsteps and incarceration quickly followed.

Keith was in and out of borstal as a teenager and, as an

adult, did time in Brixton prison for robbery. A period on the straight and narrow ensued, and he studied for his A levels in Bromley Technical Institute whilst dating the love of his life. He was subsequently devastated when he split with his girl-friend, and headed to London where he lived rough for a time. Down on his luck, but desperate to make an honest go of things, he was assisted by a voluntary charity, Teamwork Associates, in putting the jigsaw of his life back together. As luck would have it, he was assisted by Lady Pamela Onslow, one of the organisation's volunteers, who was also a Ministry of Defence official and mixed in the finest circles of Tory-dom. She was the daughter of the Nineteenth Viscount Dillon of Rath House, in Termonfeckin, County Louth, and her late husband was Tory Assistant Chief Whip in the House of Lords. She also counted amongst her friends Lord Carring-ton, the British Minister of Defence.

Lady Pamela's acquaintance with Keith Littlejohn coin-cided with the arrival in London of his big brother. When Kenneth heard of Lady Onslow, his opportunism led him to devise a plan. Using Keith as an intermediary, he got word to Lady Pamela that he had information on IRA activities in Ire-land that could be of great use to the Ministry of Defence, and indeed to the defence of the realm. Capitalising on the cold-war situation, he fabricated a story that he had been shown Russian AK49 Kalashnikov rifles in County Galway, a cache of which been landed there by Russian submarines. His intimate knowledge of Bond movies was suddenly becoming useful. He intimated to Lady Onslow that he would only disclose his knowledge of IRA activities to a min-ister whose face he would recognise from the television.

BREAK-OUT!

Lady Onslow did arrange a meeting in her home at Calcott Street, Kensington, between Kenneth and a Crown minister, in this instance a junior minister in the Department of Defence called Geoffrey Johnson Smith.

During their three-hour meeting, Kenneth described how he had made significant contacts with active republicans in County Kerry, which was a hotbed of republicanism at the time. As further evidence of his seamless integration into republican circles, he told them that he was made aware of plans to assassinate the Junior Minister for Home Affairs in Stormont, John Taylor. Furthermore, he claimed that he also knew the location of arms dumps and was able to plumb the sympathies of some prominent members of the Fianna Fáil government. Johnson Smith was sufficiently impressed with the information being offered by Kenneth to offer to put him in touch with the Special Branch.

Kenneth had enjoyed sufficient dealings with the police to know that Branchmen were still policemen, and therefore not to be trusted. He was no longer in the criminal realm, but that of international espionage, and so he insisted that he would deal only with military intelligence. At the end of the meeting, Johnson Smith said he would get in touch with the appropriate authorities. The very next day Kenneth had a meeting with the man from MI6 who was to become his spymaster, Douglas Smythe (whose real name was John Wyman). They struck a deal. The charges against Kenneth in England would be dropped in return for his co-operation. As far as Kenneth was concerned, he was now like one of the *corps diplomatique*, immune from prosecution. He couldn't be touched, no matter what murky waters he would have to wade in.

The British establishment had enjoyed a peaceful few dec-ades in Northern Ireland, but with the civil rights movement in the North gathering momentum, they began to realise that their information on the enemy was not what it should be. Soon after agreeing to intern republicans in 1971 at the behest of the Stormont government, the British realised that much of Stormont's intelligence was hopelessly outdated; many of those interned were inactive, or the son of somebody who had been active in the fifties. The British required their own operatives on the ground, but inevitably there was conflict between MI5 and MI6 as to which organisation should be overseeing intelligence operations in Ireland. MI5 was in charge of domestic intelligence, while MI6's role was for operations outside the UK, and there was some confusion as to where Northern Ireland stood in this regard, so for a time both organisations were operating in the province. But it was clear that they badly needed to infiltrate these insurgent organisations, and they needed plausible infiltrators.

While the authorities were trying to keep a lid on affairs in Northern Ireland after Bloody Sunday, the Official IRA staged a bungled revenge bomb attack on the paratroopers' head-quarters in Aldershot, killing seven people on 22 February 1972. An army chaplain was the closest thing to a legitimate target, as the other victims comprised five cleaners and a gar-dener. This led MI6 to step up espionage activity in Ireland in earnest and establish their 'Irish squad'. Of the two republi-can organisations, the Provisional and the Official IRA, the Officials were believed to be the more dangerous, as they were hell-bent on overthrowing the state. The communist threat they posed was considered more threatening in this time of cold-war espionage, and the smuggling of Russian-made weaponry by submarines was of particular concern. Who was best placed to infiltrate this threat? When a botched assassination attempt on John Taylor occurred, it enhanced Kenneth's credibility and he was considered to be a good man for the job.

Smythe briefed Kenneth for his mission (should he choose to accept it). He was to infiltrate the Officials along the border region, and obtain information about cross-border activity there. In the South, he was to act as an *agent provocateur* and stir up public opinion against the IRA Officials, thus forcing the government to enact more draconian legislation against these terrorists. So began Kenneth's life as an MI6 spy. Smythe issued him with the telephone number of Detective Inspector Sinclair of the Special Branch, whom he was to contact should he run into any difficulties with the police. He was also provided with an ex-directory number of MI6's London office.

Travel between Ireland and Britain, which at the time was subject to very tight security, would be afforded to both the Littlejohns. They scheduled a number of meetings in Dublin and Belfast, where Kenneth was to provide regular updates on progress. According to Kenneth himself, he was instructed by his spymaster to assassinate Seán Mac Stiofáin, the Chief of Staff of the Provos, as well as both Sean Garland and Seamus Costello of the Official movement. Kenneth makes the startling claim that his spymaster told him to 'disintegrate' Mac Stiofáin after 'taking' him at his home. This meant that Kenneth was to execute the IRA leader, bury his body secretly, and park his car at Dublin airport. MI6 would arrange for regular cheque payments to be sent to Mac Stiofáin's family from Canada, while circulating the story that he had absconded with IRA funds.

According to a third brother, both Littlejohns were now in the employ of the state with an annual salary of £5,000 per year, quite a substantial sum then. When Kenneth landed in Dublin he stayed in Buswell's and the Wicklow hotels, from where he began the dangerous game of espionage and infiltration. Throughout 1972 he had frequent meetings with Smythe in Dublin, Belfast and Newry. At one of them, apparently, his spymaster became misty-eyed. 'You know, Ken,' he said, 'this is no life, you get tired of it. Don't you feel you would like to give it up and go home and buy yourself a little shop?' 'I can't ever see myself selling sweets or groceries to anyone,' Kenneth replied. 'It's my type of life and I believe in what I am doing.'

He was determined to do enough to justify the British dropping the charges against him, but where to start? He did his research on both the Provisionals and the Officials, but soon found that initial contacts were wary of him; his Land Rover and English accent didn't inspire solidarity. He was finding his initial forays into espionage as difficult as his business endeavours in the hot-pants fiasco and he needed to prove his worth, as he was constantly getting the cold shoulder. He knew that he and his brother would make a more formidable team, and would have the advantage of 'safety in numbers', so he summoned him to Ireland. In the spring of 1972, Kenneth was joined by Keith and they moved to a housing estate in Rostrevor, in County Down, where they led extravagant lives, driving fast cars, sipping expensive wines and attracting the attentions of numerous women. They surprised and delighted their bank manager with occasional large deposits. With their big ideas and flamboyant swagger, their spymaster was concerned that they were a little too conspicuous for safety's sake, and that he was losing his grasp on the pair. For their part, the Littlejohns had now fulfilled their ambition of living a highflying life on Her Majesty's secret service.

Finally they made a breakthrough and established a meaningful connection. They had a relative in the army who was married to a girl in Rostrevor, and her sister was the wife of a senior member of the IRA Officials in south Down. When introduced, the Littlejohns maintained that they shared a common enemy with the republicans, as they too were wanted by British police for their lavish bank heists. They now mixed freely with both Officials and Provisionals in the bars and clubs in south Down, south Armagh and Louth, with their ears pricked for loose talk. It was not long before they had duped the local Official IRA into believing their credentials, and when they displayed their prowess for knocking off banks, their integration was seamless.

On 29 May 1972, the Official IRA declared a cease-fire, that was not accepted by the south Down Officials keen to continue with the struggle. Paul Tinnely was the head of the south Down Officials at the time; a military man from Rostrevor, he was increasingly disillusioned with the socialist tendencies of the Officials and continued fighting with a dissident unit, known locally as 'The Pimpernels'. As Official strictures were no longer in place, the group took to raiding banks for their own personal gain. As they were now involved with a splinter group, the Littlejohns were cut off from the Officials, but were in too deep to pull back. They had to continue with their activities or their cover would be blown. So far, they had succeeded in stringing along both their spymaster and this motley crew of renegades, but the stakes were rising all the time. To their spymaster, the Littlejohns were becoming a liability. They were on the fringes of a tearaway group whose activities were more criminal than political, and they certainly weren't delivering the beef.

The brothers spent their time between Rostrevor and Clogher Head where, to give them an air of respectability, Kenneth's wife Christine joined them in a house called Smuggler's Cottage. They socialised freely with republicans in the Big Tree pub, hoping to garner information that would be useful to their employers. They drove an E-type Jaguar, along with a Triumph Spitfire, and they boasted to all and sundry of their sophisticated social circles in England. Behind this mask of lah-de-dah respectability, the Littlejohns were deeply involved with the Pimpernels around the time they carried out bank robberies in Rostrevor, Warrenpoint and Newry.

Their spymaster, Douglas Smythe, knew that he had unleashed a monster in the Littlejohns, but he was reluctant to put a stop to their gallop as he still thought that they could be useful as *agents provocateurs*. He could see the ambivalence of southern politicians towards republicans, and felt some of them required a taste of their own medicine with a dose of violence south of the border. To this end, he instructed the brothers to stir up some mayhem in County Louth. On 22 September, they carried out petrol-bomb attacks on Garda stations in the towns of Castlebellingham and Louth. At the same time trouble spilt onto the streets of Dundalk when a riot broke out and angry mobs attacked a Garda station. The army had to intervene as the crowds besieged the fire-brigade vehicles. This level of unrest provoked Desmond O'Malley, the then Minister for Justice in Ireland, to introduce new and tougher anti-terrorist amendments to the Offences Against the State Act. For this, the Littlejohns can claim some responsibility. In addition, Smythe's spy ring in Ireland received a boost when he made contact with an informer in the Garda Síochána, Detective Sergeant Patrick Crinnion. In his role as a clerical officer in the Branch's terrorism and subversion division C3, Crinnion had access to highly sensitive files on the IRA, which he began passing on to Smythe.

Because he had tapped into a source of superior information, Smythe was replaced as the Littlejohn's agent by a person they were to know only as 'Oliver'. This 'spook' was a harder taskmaster than Smythe: he was very demanding on the brothers, and suspected them of being out for their own gain when results were not forthcoming. To Kenneth, this Oliver was straight out of public school and afraid of getting his hands dirty. He later stated: 'This guy had the queen's regulations shoved up his ass.' Oliver wanted the results of illegal acts but without the acts themselves. Kenneth insisted that eggs needed to be broken in order to make omelettes, and they argued constantly. Kenneth needed somebody who would dig him out if he was in the shit, and this guy couldn't be relied upon. All meetings were conducted in an atmosphere of suspicion and mistrust, entirely different from his contacts with his former boss, and soon communication broke down between the agents and their master. The Little-johns had now snapped their leash.

Kenneth could see the writing on the wall. He knew he wasn't coming up with the goodies required by MI6, but mistrustful republicans were stonewalling his efforts at any meaningful infiltration. It was only a matter of time before they discovered his true allegiance and this could have dire, even deadly, consequences. He was spinning too many plates, and sooner or later one would come crashing to the floor. Where could he turn? He had no future here, and felt that it was time to go legit again. It was around this time that he renewed his acquaintance with his former business partner Robert Stockman, who approached him about buying a restaurant in Torquay, which they would convert into a chip shop. However, Stockman lacked the cash to make the purchase, and the Littlejohns weren't exactly rolling in it either, so Kenneth came up with a double whammy, which would solve all their problems with one bold stroke.

The Pimpernels would raid the Bank of Ireland on Park Street in Dundalk, which, in addition to stirring up trouble in the South, would net a few bob for the restaurant purchase. The bank raid was scheduled for 4 October 1972, to coincide with the appearance of sixteen men in the Special Criminal Court charged with street disturbances during Dundalk's riot. The props for the job were arranged – dark blue business suits, hats, false beards, suitcases, holdalls and five handguns. It was to be an early-morning raid and they were to address each other by their pre-assigned military titles: Major, Captain, Corporal, Sergeant and Private.

BREAK-OUT!

Kenneth was first on the scene and rounded up the only staff on duty, a porter and a cleaning lady. The porter was quite compliant, but Kenneth feared a mop to the back of the head when his back was turned on the cleaning lady. Keith and the rest of the gang arrived and set to work. There was another woman in the basement who had to be held hostage, and Kenneth left one of the men to guard her with the words: 'Look after Marilyn Monroe, Corporal.' As the rest of the staff arrived for work, the porter was to admit them and they were each to be captured. However, the first of them to arrive immediately spotted a gun, panicked and ran back into the street. The gang also panicked and abandoned the raid, fretful that they wouldn't get away 'clean'. They arrived at the getaway cars, a Fiat and Kenneth's English-registered Ford, to discover that the gang was one short, as they'd forgotten their 'Corporal' in the basement. They went back to retrieve him before the alarm was raised, and managed to get away. The raid was an embarrassing fiasco from start to finish, and they accused one another of botching it. As it turned out, it was merely a dress rehearsal for a bigger show the following week.

▲▲▲

Kenneth awoke beside his wife on Thursday, 12 October 1972. This was the big one. As well as Keith, who had gone to England after the previous job but had returned specially for this one, five other Pimpernels men were on hand. After many reconnaissance missions, Littlejohn had observed that the AIB Bank on Dublin's Grafton Street, right in the heart of the capital, was a sitting duck. Keith had already reconnoitred the manager's home, posing as an encyclopaedia salesman. At

8.00am on that fateful Thursday, bank manager Noel Curran opened the door of his Lower Kilmacud Road home to an urgent knocking. Three men carrying pistols burst through the door shouting 'Get inside', and forced their way into the bedroom where Curran's wife, Mona, lay in bed. One of the raiders stood at the foot of the bed with his pistol, intimidating them into compliance by taking a bullet from his pocket, holding it in front of him, and saying: 'This is a dumdum bullet. It makes a nice clean hole.' The dumdum is a vicious little soft-nosed bullet that expands on impact. They proceeded to tie up Mona, her sister, and two children, Hugh (10) and Neal (4).

In the middle of all this, Hugh inquired, 'Is this a hold-up?' and excitedly asked his mother if they would require treatment for shock afterwards. As the house was settling into a calm hijack situation the milkman arrived with his delivery, and a momentary sense of panic gripped the raiders. However, he didn't notice anything untoward. Afterwards the family was held hostage in the garage, while Curran was instructed to help the other men rob his bank. They were left in the care of an armed man who wore a blue J-cloth over his mouth. Bizarrely, neither Kenneth nor Keith made any effort to conceal themselves, even though the pair were so striking-looking that if they were merely entering a bank and cashing a cheque, any self-respecting female teller would be able to pick them out of a crowd. As they drove to the bank in Curran's marigold-coloured Hillman Hunter, Kenneth said to Curran: 'It's time this part of the country got a taste of its own medicine.' Curran was instructed to co-operate fully with the raiders or there would be unhappy consequences for his family. He opened the bank, and the raiders were joined by another man carrying a large carpenter's toolbox, obviously for the loot. They set to work like soldiers, addressing each other with the titles of 'Major', 'Captain' and 'Corporal'. Kenneth was the Major, of course. By this stage the staff of the bank were arriving for duty, and needed to be admitted in order not to arouse suspicion. All twenty-two staff were admitted by Curran himself, and were subsequently locked in the vault.

The assistant manager, Gordon Simpson, arrived for work only to encounter the raiders. Thinking it to be a joke, he brandished his umbrella at one of them. He was swiftly pushed against the wall and a gun put to his head with the hammer cocked. He quickly realised that these boys were no actors. Apart from this incident, the staff were well treated and the raid had a certain *élan*. One of the girls complained to Kenneth that the heating was not turned on and that they were cold. He ordered the porter, Hartigan, to make tea for all and gave them makeshift seats, made of ledgers, to sit upon. As the raid progressed the raiders chatted casually with staff about the Joe Bugner boxing match that had been televised the previous night. Another conversation meandered to the subject of the poor telephone system in the South.

At 10.30am, outside the bank, irate customers were forming a queue, wondering why it had not yet opened. The Gardaí were called and forced an entrance. Half an hour earlier, having hoovered up the sterling and Irish bank notes on the premises, the gang had made their getaway. The raiders, numbering six in total, got away with

IR£67,000, at the time the largest amount ever taken in a bank raid in the history of the Republic. Throughout the robbery the Littlejohns made no attempt to hide their faces, left their fingerprints all over the bank, and Kenneth even left a utility bill, under his pseudonym Kenneth Austen but with an address in Achill Court in Drumcondra, in the getaway car they abandoned in the carpark of Dublin airport. Once he received word that the raid had been carried off successfully, their accomplice in the Curran household hijacked Mrs Curran's humble brown mini and made off, abandoning it on Stephen's Green.

The Littlejohns, along with Kenneth's wife Christine, made their way to London, thinking their tasks as *agents provocateurs* had been well and truly accomplished. Into the bargain, Kenneth would have enough cash to go halves with Stockman on the purchase of the Torquay restaurant and put this duplicitous life behind him. Four days after the robbery, Gardaí found £5,000 in Kenneth's Drumcondra flat, but they still didn't know what he looked like. They had nothing on this Austen person, but further investigation led them to Kerry's Farranfore airport. Following the trail of the hot-pants company, Whizz Kids, they encountered Kennelly, who still had the photograph of Austen/Littlejohn that he had taken to make into a poster. The Branch now knew who they were seeking.

A week later, on 19 October, with his wife and a close circle of friends, Kenneth celebrated his birthday in Stockman's house, drinking a toast to their new life as restaurateurs. That same day he had met with Oliver beneath the statue of Nelson in Trafalgar Square, and passed on his last shreds of information to him. He arrived with an Ordnance Survey map of the south Down area, and Kenneth marked on it the location of an IRA arms dump. Oliver proceeded to tell Kenneth that he had gone too far with the bank raid and that he could be extradited to face charges. Kenneth argued that he needed to engage in such activity in order not to blow his cover, but his entreaties were falling on increasingly deaf ears. 'It's a bit late, you telling me that now I'll be extradited,' Kenneth said at the end of their long meeting. 'I'll go back to them and see what I can do,' replied Oliver, 'and we'll talk tomorrow. In the meantime, keep your head down.' Later that day Kenneth was picked up by the Flying Squad, Scotland Yard's elite anti-crime unit, along with his wife and his associate Robert Stockman, and brought to Edgware police station in Middlesex.. A key to a safety deposit box in a Regent Street bank was found in Stockman's home, and on investigation was found to have £11,000 in Irish notes in it. That same day, Keith was arrested in Torquay, where police found £5,000 and some hand-guns. On arrival at the station Kenneth told his arresting officer to contact Inspector Sinclair, and gave him the contact number provided by his former spymaster Smythe/Wyman. The number was no longer in service, and it seemed the same could be said for the Littlejohns. Inspector Parker finally told them: 'Right, you are going to be shipped out to Ireland.' 'Not on your life,' said Kenneth, but Parker stood firm. Having now outlived their usefulness, they were being left unprotected to face the music.

All the while, Smythe/Wyman was extracting valuable information from Patrick Crinnion in the Irish Special

Branch. Slowly but surely, however, Crinnion's colleagues in the branch were closing a net around him. On 21 December, he went to meet Smythe/Wyman in the Burlington hotel in Dublin, but was instead greeted by a number of his colleagues from the Branch, and a quick search under the carpeting in his car revealed a file of documents marked 'classified'. They were obviously intended for the spymaster, but unbeknownst to Crinnion, the day before their meeting Smythe/Wyman had been picked up by the Gardaí in the West County hotel in Chapelizod, where he admitted to being a British secret agent.

The Irish government was demanding that the brothers be extradited to face charges for the Dublin bank raid, and the British needed to rescue their spymaster Smythe/Wyman. The British and Irish struck a deal whereby the Littlejohns' extradition was conditional on their trial being criminal and not political in nature. The Crinnion and Smythe/Wyman case opened *in camera* in Dublin on 1 February 1973. Because the Attorney General requested that top-secret documents be deemed inadmissible as evidence, Crinnion and Smythe/Wyman were found guilty of summary charges only, and sentenced to three months' imprisonment dating from the time of their arrests, a sentence which had since elapsed. They were therefore free men, flew to London together on 13 February, and then vanished. Crinnion is thought to be living in exile.

The day before their extradition case was to open, the Littlejohns asked their solicitor, Peter Hughman, to issue witness summonses to Lord Carrington, Geoffrey Johnson Smith, Lady Pamela Onslow, and Douglas Smythe. When the hearing started, the British attorney general applied for the case to be heard *in camera*, and his wish was granted. The extradition case opened in Bow Street Magistrate's Court and Kenneth, Keith, Christine Littlejohn and Robert Stockman appeared in front of Lord Widgery. Their requests for witnesses were not granted and there was no mention of military intelligence in the proceedings. The judge deemed the Dublin robbery to be criminal in nature, and the court backed up the Irish warrant and ordered that Robert Stockman and the Littlejohn brothers, but not Christine, were to be returned to Dublin to face charges. Stockman was also wanted for questioning in connection with a £13,000 raid on the Hillgrove hotel in north Monaghan, in addition to harbouring a criminal (Littlejohn). Littlejohn was aghast. He knew the British government couldn't assist them openly, but he had always trusted that behind the scenes a backroom deal could be done and that the British would do the right thing by them. It was the least they could do after he had risked life and limb for them. But the Littlejohns were left swinging in an icy wind by their former employers. They had obviously meant it when they explained the first rule of espionage: If you're caught, you're on your own.

They were duly extradited on 19 March 1973. At the opening of the Dublin trial in the Special Criminal Court, Kenneth stated that he thought that Jesus Christ had had a better chance of a fair hearing. He also claimed that Littlejohn was an assumed name, and that his actual name was Kenneth Austen, but the reverse was proven to be the case. The Littlejohns made several attempts to refer to the political nature of their activity in Ireland, which were ruled out of order. The court was only interested in their criminal involvement in the bank raid, and found that Kenneth could only explain the whereabouts of a fraction of the £67,000 that had been stolen. When Kenneth was sentenced to twenty years' penal servitude for his part in the robbery, he shouted from the dock: 'Thank you, England – ask Lord Carrington what he thinks of that lot.' Keith got fifteen years, but Stockman was acquitted. Back in Torquay, Christine Littlejohn picked up the phone and dialled 2301212, extension 2118, which was the number Kenneth had given her for his spymaster – Douglas Smythe/John Wyman. The switchboard operator put her on hold for an agonising moment. When she finally returned, she said 'Sorry, but we have no Douglas here.' Christine slammed the phone down in a fury. So much for the promised immunity! The Littlejohns' use-by date had now definitely expired.

When Keith arrived in Mountjoy prison's B2 wing, news of his activities as a British spy had reached the Official IRA prisoners already there, and they formed a welcoming committee: a few of them tried to string up the British *agent provocateur* in his cell, but Keith managed to foil the attack by fighting off his assailants and alerting the authorities. Both brothers were transferred to the basement of B wing, which was reserved for inmates who were at risk from the other prisoners. For their own safety, the brothers were confined to solitary for twenty-three hours a day, and there was a permanent guard outside their cell door. After some time, they were able to broker a truce with the republican prisoners and were left unharmed. Although it has the capacity for some thirty-five prisoners, they had the 'base', as it is known, practically to themselves (with the exception of three loyalist prisoners and some sex offenders). Here they were afforded quite a bit of privacy and lived lives in prison almost akin to political status. While other male prisoners had to wear prison clothes, the brothers wore civilian clothing all the time. They were permitted to carry an attaché case, which the prison officers were instructed not to search. The Littlejohns managed to persuade the naive authorities that this case contained their political papers. It did, but it also contained their hacksaw blades.

On 13 August 1973, Jack Lynch admitted that when he was Taoiseach he had received a diplomatic dossier through the London embassy stating that the Littlejohns had been used as British agents in Ireland. This was grist to the mill for the Littlejohns, who appealed the Special Criminal Court's sentence. But by early 1974 Kenneth became increasingly despondent that the normal channels were going to secure his release, and turned his attention to escaping. His adrenalin-fuelled addiction to danger meant he could never rest in a place like this. After scrutinising the prison routine, he discovered the ideal time for an escape bid was between 7.00 and 7.30 in the evening, while the prisoners were taking exercise. If an escape were to be attempted, it had to be done before the beginning of summer time when clocks went forward and the days became longer. The Littlejohns were still waiting on the results of an appeal to the Supreme Court, but as this was not forthcoming they decided to break out rather than wait on the outcome.

Kenneth exploited the prison officers' respect for religion.

When he told them that he was practising yoga, they often left him to his own devices, thinking it to be a cultist religion. Also, he declared that he was frustrated with being treated as a criminal and embarked on a hunger strike, demanding political status and more frequent visits from his wife. Keith vowed to continue the strike should his brother die. This turned out not to be for political purposes, but in order to be able to fit through the window bars he was sawing through whilst ostensibly doing his yoga. Kenneth needed to slim down from his current fourteen stone to a trimmer eleven. The Littlejohns were at sufficient liberty to erect their own gymnasium in the 'base' and they honed their boxing skills, and no doubt aided their slimming efforts, with a punchbag suspended from the ceiling. This was also a useful medium for Kenneth to vent his frustration at the situation in which he now found himself, although a glance up, from his punchbag to the gymnasium window, would show the progress he was making on the window bar. The punchbag served another purpose: in it they hid the rope they had made from blankets, which they planned to use in their escape.

They had decided to make their bid for freedom on Monday, 11 March, in the final week of daylight-saving time. The time to move was 7.00pm, as this was when the warders would be at their busiest on the evening shift and could be caught unawares. But at 6.30pm they learnt to their horror that they had a visit from their lawyer, William Blood Smyth. It seemed to take the warders an age to lead them to the visiting room, and they tried as nonchalantly as possible to conduct a normal conversation with one eye on the clock. They managed to wrap up their conversation in fifteen minutes, which meant the window of opportunity was still ajar.

Some prisoners were watching television while others were being served their supper and cocoa in their cells. According to Kenneth, unbeknownst to the warders he and Keith slipped through the sawn-through gap in the window with some ease, and made their way to the perimeter wall of the prison. However, three prison warders were subsequently fined after the event, and there is some speculation that the escape may have been internally assisted. The bar in the window was indeed cut, but the gap was very narrow for a grown man to squeeze through, even one who was on hunger strike. Assuming they didn't go through the bars, in order for them to have reached the yard they would have had to get past the guard on their door, another guard at the entrance to the B wing basement, and down a tunnel to a third gate that was also manned and supposedly locked. The guards were either not there, or not looking. Once the brothers had made it to the yard, they attached a weight to the blanket rope and slung it over the wall, but even after many attempts it simply didn't catch.

They continued along the perimeter wall to some scaffolding, where labourers had been working on an interior wall. They took four planks, which measured twenty feet in total, to the perimeter wall and assembled them into a makeshift ramp, which left them within reach of the top of the wall. Climbing the scaffolding to get the planks had caused such a racket that the prison officers were now running to foil the escape bid. Kenneth climbed on Keith's head to get sufficient purchase to grip the top of the wall, and was able to pull himself on to it. In pulling Keith up, they knocked over the makeshift ramp, sending it crashing to the ground. There was still a massive drop to negotiate on the other side. Taking off his denim jacket, Kenneth suspended his little brother down the outer perimeter. Keith gripped the sleeve of the jacket, but just as he was about to drop, the jacket spun him around and he fell awkwardly. He rolled over, clutching his ankle and writhing in agony. After his own leap down, Kenneth picked him up and they made their way through the narrow laneways onto Glengariff Parade, brothers in arms.

As they made their way towards Drumcondra, a great big bear of a warder called Willy Barrett was returning from work, and spotted the two brothers making their getaway. He couldn't believe his eyes, and leapt from his car and tried to apprehend them. The brothers scarpered, but Keith was caught after a short pursuit as he simply could not run. He was returned to the prison. Kenneth ran through a side door of McGrath's pub, then out through the front entrance onto Dorset Street, where he sprang on to a passing bus heading northwards, out of the city. He suspected that he had been spotted by Gardaí when boarding the bus, so he got off in Drumcondra after a short journey.

It was a good move because immediately after he alighted, the bus was stopped and searched by the Gardaí. Kenneth made his way to Corpus Cristi church, but found it to be locked. The night was bitterly cold, and frost was forming on the ground. He discovered a hatch, which led to an underground boiler room, and thought he would find warmth in there. Surely they needed a large boiler to heat this huge church. He tried in vain to get the boiler working, but finally gave up, hid himself and fell into a deep sleep, only to be awoken the next morning by the church's oil delivery. The oil pipes were rolled in to the boiler room while Kenneth squatted out of view. Discovery would prove disastrous. To his relief, the oil man eventually packed up his hoses and went away. Kenneth was about to leave when he heard the same guy approaching again, and he quickly hid underneath the boiler, which was damp and dripping with filthy oil.

As he lay there, in a pool of water and oil, six workmen and the priest tried to fix the boiler, which they finally managed to do by 6.00pm. Kenneth clambered out from under the boiler, which was now quite toasty, and stripped off, hanging his clothes on the metal surface to dry. He sat there, waiting for night time before he dared to venture outside, as he knew that a manhunt was well and truly underway at this stage. He heard footsteps outside, and grabbed his clothes and hid once more, but it was just the bloody priest checking on his precious boiler. When all was to his satisfaction he left, and Kenneth decided it was now time to leave the boiler house. He made his way to Howth, where he built a bivouac of sticks and ferns and lived on Howth Head for two nights. His intention was to make his way to Northern Ireland, from where he could return to friends in England. At least across the border they would have to go through the extradition proceedings again, and he would be able to plead his case that he had been engaged as a British spy.

He made his way steadily northwards but hunger and

unfamiliar surroundings quickly left him disorientated. He spent the night in a shed in the backyard of a house. Imagine his horror the following day when he awoke to discover that he was a stone's throw from Mountjoy again. He had gone full circle. On subsequent nights he followed railway tracks until he got to County Louth. For a couple of nights he lived in a beach hut near Termonfeckin, close to the ancestral home of Lady Onslow, the woman through whom he had embarked on this phase of his life. With money he had brought out of prison with him, he bought a pair of shoes and an anorak in Drogheda and managed to wash his clothes in seawater, scrubbing them with seaweed. He was now moving in fairly familiar territory, and caught a train into Dundalk, booking himself into the Imperial hotel masquerading as a German tourist named Karl Heckman. Residing in room nine, Herr Heckman did not speak any English and barked at the staff in German. After a couple of nights as Heckman, he shaved his head, donned a slightly bedraggled overcoat and hat, and worked on hobbling like an old man. Dressed in such finery, he boarded a train in Dundalk and made his way across the border to Belfast. It was simple in the end. In Belfast he teamed up with friends who took him to the Larne ferry, and ultimately he made his way through Britain to Amsterdam. As the Dutch would not extradite somebody to a non-jury court, which is what the Special Criminal Court in Dublin was, he could stop running. He was safe there.

▲▲▲

On 2 June 1974, Paul Tinnely was gunned down by an M1 carbine by his own people, the Official IRA, on his doorstep in

BREAK-OUT!

Rostrevor, County Down. As he was suspected of feeding information to the British through the Littlejohns, Keith Littlejohn wrote a letter to Tinnelly's family from Mountjoy prison refuting this. For what it was worth to the family, he stated that Tinnely had never been compromised by the Littlejohns and was always loyal to the republican cause. Still suspicious of her role in the affair, the provisional IRA sent the unsolicited gift of a book to Lady Onslow in 1982. Concealed within its pages was a two-pound bomb which, thankfully for her, failed to detonate.

Twenty months after his successful escape, Kenneth was re-arrested in London and once again extradited to Dublin, to serve out the remainder of his original sentence in the bowels of B Wing. That same year, the brothers made another unsuccessful escape attempt. Because of their previous bid for freedom, the authorities could not contemplate another embarrassing break-out and they were very closely guarded. A special observation post was erected overlooking the brothers' cells, and it is known to this day as 'The Littlejohn Box'. Every second Sunday, the Littlejohns attended a private church service, and on one particular day, they bound and gagged the pastor, Arnold Perdue, and erected barricades, more in the hope of drawing attention to their plight than a genuine escape attempt. After a short siege, they were overpowered by the warders, and failed to attract any attention to their situation as their newsworthiness had long since faded.

The brothers were released early in 1981 for health reasons, on condition that they leave Ireland forever. At 4.00am, under cover of darkness, the Littlejohns were escorted to the border and handed over to the British, who flew them by helicopter back to England. Back on home turf, Kenneth inevitably returned to his old ways and was jailed for six years, in Winston Green prison, for his part in an armed robbery in Chesterfield. The brothers renewed their threats to expose the British government's spying activity by writing a tell-all book about their exploits, but this never materialised.

The Wooden Horse of Long Kesh

THE PRISON OFFICER SHOWED the new internee his new home; home for God knows how long. He had just landed in the Long Kesh internment camp. The IRA OC of the camp greeted him, but there was no time wasted with lavish welcomes. 'There's a move on here,' the rookie was told, 'we're making an escape bid tonight and we need you on the outside.' He was already part of an escape attempt!

A loyal and diligent IRA volunteer, the rookie was ready for whatever it took. The plan was that he would hide in a refuse sack until he was lifted to a secure location. 'When I give the signal,' the OC told him, 'you're to run like fuck away from the noise as fast as your legs will take you. You'll be met on the outside, don't worry.' He was helped into the plastic bag, which was tied at the top but had enough air coming in to enable him to breathe comfortably. His nostrils filled with the putrid smell of rotting cabbage, and time passed. His legs were aching from crouching in the same position for so long, and he wondered would he be able to run. Would his legs buckle under his weight? After what seemed an eternity, the bag was lifted and he was carried outside by an unwitting helper. Again he waited, ears pricked for the signal, his legs itching to start moving again. The signal came. Freedom beckoned. He leapt out and started to run, but stopped quickly. All around him were prisoners and prison officers, pointing and laughing. It was a ready-up. All he could do was smile. You're in the army now, he thought.

▲▲▲

For the prisoners, Long Kesh was to escaping what Mount Everest is to climbing. It began life as an internment camp made up of Nissen huts, called 'cages' by the prisoners, but in the seventies was transformed into a full-fledged prison, called the Maze. Throughout the seventies, before its trans-formation, the prison was a penitential sieve and escape was an integral part of its culture. Every conceivable means of getting out was explored. In November 1974 Hugh Coney was shot dead by the army as he emerged from a tunnel and the escape of the thirty-one men behind him was foiled. Such was the tunnelling activity that at one time republicans almost burrowed into a loyalist tunnel.

Although lacking the same culture of escapes that republi-cans possessed, some loyalists were equally determined to make a break for it. A UVF man called McRea almost made it out by clinging to the bottom of a transport lorry, hanging on for dear life for the best part of a day. He was caught at the final gate. Another, Benny Redfern, hid in a bin that was to be carried out of the prison on 9 August 1974. He was crushed to death by the teeth of the bin lorry when he was cast into it.

On 9 September 1973 Fr Gerry Green came into the com-pound to say Mass for the prisoners. As he served Communion, the prisoners noticed that he bore a remarkable resemblance to one of the prisoners, John Francis Green. This was more than mere coincidence, though, as they were brothers. When Fr Green was escorted from the prison, he bade the officers farewell and said he would be back the following Sunday. He was never seen again. His brother, the real Fr Green, was found bound and gagged inside the prison. Two other republican prisoners were to escape dressed as priests from the Kesh in the seventies.

But another struggle was to put thoughts of escaping to the back of prisoners' minds for some time. In 1976 the government was pursuing a policy of 'criminalisation' whereby the special-category status enjoyed by political prisoners since the outbreak of the Troubles was denied them. Long Kesh internment camp became HMP Maze, though republicans insisted on continuing to call it Long Kesh, 'The Cages' or 'The Blocks'. Under the new regime they would have to wear prison uniforms and do prison work. 'Even if they were to nail that prison uniform to my back, I wouldn't wear it,' was the cry of defiance uttered by Ciarán Nugent when the prison authorities tried to force him to wear a prison uniform in 1976. He was the first to lose special-category status and to be treated like a common criminal, and went on the 'blanket protest' to assert his political status. He would go naked, draped in a blanket, sooner than wear a criminal uniform. As the protest intensified others joined him and the 'dirty protest' commenced. Prisoners would smear their excrement on the cell walls rather than be forced to walk naked to the bathrooms. The dirty protest proved to be counter-productive: it failed to achieve any concessions and served only to reinforce racial stereotyping of the Irish living like animals. The protest had to be taken a step further. When Bobby Sands, OC in the prison, and his comrades embarked on their fateful hunger strikes in 1981 in order to assert their political status, they cast around for somebody to manage the hunger strikes, and they selected Brendan McFarlane because they knew him to be an unflinching commander, unafraid to let them die for the cause. In all, ten men died on hunger strike. Two years later, on 22 September 1983, McFarlane was to play another leading role in the history of HMP Maze. While he was OC, a staggering thirty-eight IRA prisoners managed to break out of what was then considered to be the most secure prison in Western Europe.

▲▲▲

McFarlane had grown up in the Catholic Ardoyne area of north Belfast. Because north Belfast has a mixed population of Catholics and Protestants, it is perhaps the most sectarianised area of the city. McFarlane's family was deeply religious and, as a teenager, he was an altar boy in the local church. At seventeen, he decided to follow his vocation and joined a missionary school in Wales, studying to be a priest. In all, he spent a couple of years there, but when he came home on holidays he saw that his people were under siege in the enclave of Ardoyne and there was nobody to protect them. McFarlane decided that these people didn't need spirituality, they needed to be armed, to defend themselves. It was God or the gun; he chose the latter and joined the Provos. In August 1975 he was arrested for a bomb and gun attack on the Bayardo bar which killed five Protestants. If it weren't for the sectarian nature of this attack, McFarlane would undoubtedly have a bigger political profile today.

When McFarlane and the prisoners called off their 217-day hunger strike at 3.15pm on Saturday, 3 October 1981, they were a beaten force. On the wrong end of a gruelling war of attrition, they had lost ten comrades and gained no concessions. It was always going to be a dangerous game of brinkmanship against such an unyielding force, and the intractable British Prime Minister, Margaret Thatcher, had achieved her victory over these murderers, bombers and gunmen, even if it was to prove a pyrrhic victory in the long term. That afternoon in the blocks, there were no cries of 'Tiocfaidh Ár Lá' ('our day will come'), the resistance cry of the IRA. This was not their day.

They had to pick themselves up off their knees over the succeeding months. They were at a low ebb, and the ten dead hunger strikers left a dreadful atmosphere hanging over the blocks. This was a constant psychological burden for the prisoners. Some felt guilty at having watched their comrades die, not having participated in the protest, and others were bitter at their fellow prisoners for not doing their share. Divisions were deep, and they had to rebuild from the ground up.

The deaths also had an effect on the prison officers, and the Northern Ireland Office (NIO) were conscious that they had to rebuild the prison system after this disturbing event. The prisoners on the dirty protest had lost all their privileges and were facing massive sentences. The NIO wanted prisoners working to earn back some of that lost remission, and they knew that this confrontational regime could not be sustained forever. If the prisoners would meet them half way, they could possibly negotiate. Furthermore, during

the protests there had been systematic intimidation of warders and numerous executions of staff on the outside. The
protests were as gruelling for the authorities as they were for
the prisoners and they would embrace any chance to
improve the situation.

▲▲▲

Certain republican groups elected to stop protesting and to
co-operate with the prison authorities, knowing it to be
easier to topple the system from within. The authorities were
pleased with this development. Needless to say, prisoners'
co-operation was quite limited. Protests continued – there
were mysterious fires in the workshops, and the garden
gnomes they were making as part of their prison work
always seemed to be missing limbs or heads! Prisoners could
work and sabotage simultaneously, but the great advantage
of ostensible co-operation was that they were now able to
study the lie of the land in the prison, to collect tools and
materials, and to plan how to use them to their advantage.
Those who had been on the dirty protest had been stuck in a
concrete block seven feet by eight feet, broken only by a
single window with reinforced concrete bars, for years on
end. To them, being out on the wing must have seemed to
be full of escape possibilities. At this stage, one of the key
concessions to be won was segregation from loyalist prisoners. It meant that they could organise themselves, live in their
own community, and plot and plan without interference.
While forced to live together, neither group was in control of
the wing, and both communities were constantly watching
their backs for an assault by the other. Integration ensured
that the warders were in control.

BREAK-OUT!

It was a tedious process to win segregation, as it required faction fighting, assaults, and bomb threats on each other to illustrate to the authorities that the two communities simply couldn't live together. Ironically, it was through working with loyalist prisoners that the issue was forced to a conclusion. The republicans were aggrieved throughout the prison struggle that they were doing all the protesting, but the loyalists also gained the achieved concessions. They were asked to pull their weight and smash up their cells in protest at mixed blocks. Though this collaboration was fraught at times, it achieved its goal surprisingly quickly. Segregation was granted and three of the blocks became exclusively republican. All these compromises increased the feasibility of an escape bid.

With increased co-operation with the prison authorities, the IRA officers in the blocks were gaining authority. The prison officers were acknowledging their command structures by negotiating with the OCs, albeit unofficially. The commanders negotiated to get obstinate prison officers stationed away from front-line duties. Finally, after years of struggle, there was a little give and take, and to the authorities' surprise the place was soon humming along nicely, without confrontations. With each concession granted, though, new possibilities presented themselves to the prisoners to weaken, however imperceptibly, the power of the authorities within the prison.

▲▲▲

For generations of republican prisoners, the struggle does not end because one has been locked up. Just because they were in prison didn't mean that they had stopped being volunteers. Some prisoners equate their personal liberty with that of Ireland's, so symbolically a personal escape attempt is also a strike for Irish freedom. They considered themselves to be prisoners of war, and therefore it was their sworn and solemn duty to escape. An ironic source of inspiration was the British soldiers in Nazi camps during World War II – the republicans even referred to the warders as the 'Germans'. If they could not win political status through hunger strikes, perhaps they could re-assert it by staging an escape. And not just an ordinary escape, but a mass break-out.

▲▲▲

Throughout the Troubles, there had been a constant game of cat and mouse between republican prisoners and the authorities. The prisoners would find cracks in the prison system through which they would escape, and the authorities would subsequently tighten security to prevent similar escapes. The 1970s were characterised by opportunistic, spur-of-the-moment escapes, sometimes with spectacular results. As the seventies progressed, the escapes were proving an embarrassment to the British government. As the prisoners got cleverer, so too did the authorities, until ultimately they built what was deemed to be an impregnable fortress: HMP Maze.

They went to phenomenal lengths to make it escape-proof. The Maze was surrounded by multiple layers of wires and walls, interspersed with watchtowers, manned, around the clock, by armed British army sentries, and prisoners were driven there in vans with blackened windows. There were eight blocks in the Maze. With over a hundred security gates, the blocks were laid out like individual prisons, each with a capacity for over a hundred prisoners, within the larger compound. Each block had four wings, A, B, C and D, which made up the vertical bars of the H layout. The horizontal bar of the H was known as the 'circle', which, as in conventional prisons, was the officers' control centre. In it was the principal officer's room, the welfare room, toilets, the officers' mess, the medical room and, crucially, the control room, which was fitted with alarms and direct lines to the Emergency Control Room (ECR). Like all self-respecting prisons, the blocks were designed to maximise the control of the officers, while at the same time minimising the threat of a take-over by prisoners.

As each wing was a mini-prison in itself, individual wings in the blocks could be sealed off with the flick of a switch. In order to get off his wing, a prisoner had to pass a manned security gate, and to gain access to the circle one had to pass through a similar gate. One left the circle the same way, and to leave the block one had to get through a large security fence which had a couple of airlock security gates in it. This too was manned. Even if one were to make it this far, one was still within the main prison compound and one would have to negotiate the Tally Lodge, the most difficult location of all. A small, single-storey building, this was the main pedestrian and vehicular access and egress point for the larger prison. Even prison officers were frisked coming and going at this point, and while vehicles were being prepared for security clearance they would wait in the airlock between two gates.

The compound itself was floodlit twenty-four hours a day and the grounds were constantly patrolled by prison officers with German Shepherd dogs. The latest technology was employed, including listening devices, sensors and all manner of strategically placed alarms. Infrared photography from overhead flights was employed to detect any tunnelling activity. Subsequent to the commando-style helicopter escape from Mountjoy, the area surrounding the prison was a strict no-fly zone and wiring was erected over the compound, which would entangle any would-be chopper mission. The nearby M1 motorway was floodlit by night, and any cars stopping on this stretch were immediately investigated and moved on. Entry, exit and moving within the prison were subject to rigorous checking and scrutiny, and security tags and passwords were required at each of the various gates. The authorities had certainly learnt from the mistakes of the past ten years. Whilst all these checks and balances were in place and well thought through, they were only as effective as the manpower employed to carry them out. This was the weakest link in the prisoners' incarceration chain and they knew it. Any bid for freedom would have to strike at the officers first.

The prisoners were busying themselves dreaming up escape attempts, and suggestions ranged from the bizarre to the unexpected. One volunteer had manufactured a costume made of cabbage leaves, in which he was going to crawl out of the compound cunningly disguised as a row of cabbages. Others planned countless tunnels, and even a hot-air balloon was suggested. It was all a bit haphazard, and would never penetrate what was boasted to be the most secure prison in Western Europe. A co-ordinated approach was required and they needed somebody to oversee it.

▲▲▲

BREAK-OUT!

Larry Marley was the cages' answer to Harry Houdini. He was nicknamed 'An Diabhal' ('the devil') as he was full of devilment. Others called him Papillon, after the legendary escapee. Like a medieval ghost, fortress walls could not keep him in. He will be remembered by history as the man who broke out of a courthouse where he was being charged with attempting to escape from prison! Early in 1975, he and a number of comrades, dressed as a British army foot patrol, had made their way towards the exit at the top end of the Long Kesh compound. None of the staff seemed to notice them until they got to the last gate, where they were spotted and arrested.

Marley was charged with attempted escape, and was due to appear in Newry courthouse on 11 March 1975, along with eleven comrades who had also made escape bids from the Kesh. In the courthouse, whilst awaiting their trial, they were kept in a holding cell. They discovered that the bars on the window of the adjoining toilet were badly rusted. While some of the prisoners set to work on the bars, another got a piece of soap from the sink and scraped the words 'Up the IRA' on the bathroom mirror. They broke the bars and, emerging into the yard, cast around for a means of scaling the thirty-foot barricade that surrounded the courthouse. Evading detection, they all scampered up an electricity transformer and over the fencing, although one prisoner called McMahon landed awkwardly and broke his leg on the far side. They hijacked a number of cars and made a beeline for the border, and all but two managed to evade re-capture.

If anybody could find a means out of the Maze, it was Marley, and he was duly appointed escape officer. He assembled around him a determined group of volunteers, many of whom, like himself, were veterans of previous escapes. To get out of the blocks required more than just serious planning and data collection, it required fresh ideas, and a whole new way of thinking. Rope ladders and tunnels were outmoded, as the authorities were steps ahead of them in that regard. All suggestions for escapes from all of the different blocks were submitted to Marley (who was in block H5) for assessment, feasibility and approval. He amassed all intelligence and observations, until it got to the stage where Marley knew more about the layout of the prison than the governor himself. He hoarded information: on the movement of staff at different times, when certain alarms in the blocks were not replaced, which posts were not manned, and so forth. From this intelligence, he discovered that there certainly were chinks in the armour, which was promising, but he had nothing concrete. He did not share his comrades' naivety, but his canny and rigorous nature made him investigate all avenues thoroughly.

▲▲▲

The prisoners in each block collected items that could prove useful, such as concrete saws, hacksaws, and little hammers. Any item of prison officer's clothing was also coveted as it would enable an escapee to impersonate a warder – having fallen foul of this before, the authorities had forbidden the wearing of blue or white shirts by prisoners. Any officers' hats that were carelessly left behind, or shirts of this colour, were stashed for future use. A skirmish was always a good opportunity to commandeer a prison officer's hat. All the while, a keen eye was kept on the lorry which delivered food to each block three times a day, seven days a week. Through their intelligence network the prisoners found out that officers often used the truck for 'homers'. Though the lorry was not supposed to leave the compound, it was often taken by an officer to help a neighbour move furniture, or for drinks deliveries to the prison officers' club.

Marley realised that this was the Achilles' heel of the prison. The lorry, like a Trojan horse, could be filled with a cargo of IRA volunteers and driven past the various security gates within the compound to the Tally Lodge, the entrance to the H-blocks themselves. From there it could travel the 1km past a British army base to the main entrance gate of the whole prison complex, to be waved through by unsuspecting prison warders. It justified the use of that old cliché, that it was 'so crazy, it might just work'. That was the plan, but there was a huge amount of preparation to be done to get to that point. In order to get the IRA volunteers on to the food lorry, there was no alternative but to take over the entire block from which the escapees would come.

Gaining control of the inside was a fundamental rationale of the escape. Because of the design of the prison, a block, in its entirety, would have to be taken under IRA control until the escape was over to ensure that the warders would not raise the alarm. This could only be done in the blocks that were fully under republican control, as the mixed blocks were too unpredictable. The idea of taking over an entire block was not a new one, but it was essential if you wanted to get out of the Maze as it was now designed. There were too many nerve centres and controls. There was only one means of doing this, but it would be tricky and would need approval at the highest level: the prisoners required guns, real guns with real ammunition. Most of the warders were ex-army boys and they knew a fake gun when they saw one. Take over a block and escape in the food lorry. It was patchy and incredible, but it was a plan.

▲▲▲

The idea was pitched to IRA camp staff, who felt that it had potential. The first decision was to choose the block from which the escape bid would be made. This operation needed cool heads. H7 was chosen and Bobby Storey, as Block OC, was to lead it, ably assisted by Gerry Kelly and Brendan McFarlane. Larry Marley in H5 was to provide them with all the necessaries. There was another practical reason for choosing H7: the block opposite it, H8, was empty for re-decoration. There was a risk that if the escape was attempted from somewhere else, it could be spotted from the adjacent block. The leaders in H7 set about investigating the practicalities of taking over their block. They needed to get key men appointed as orderlies, and this proved very easy as the authorities bent over backwards to accommodate those willing to work. This would enable the prisoners to swoop from different points simultaneously. Security needed to be gradually eroded by the prisoners to facilitate a greater freedom of movement within the block. The culture of co-operation had to be pushed to the limit to lull the warders into a false sense of security.

The prison officers were caught in the middle of a battle of wills between the republicans and the authorities. During the protests, the officers had witnessed their comrades being executed for carrying out their jobs, only to see the authorities subsequently cave in to the prisoners' demands. Was it all in vain? Why should the officers go out on a limb if they were going to be undermined in this way? This resentment towards the management permeated the everyday attitude in the blocks and contributed to a gradual apathy towards the system. In addition, prison officers were continually intimidated. When escorting a prisoner to a visit, an officer might be asked subtly about the new tricycle he had bought for his young son that Christmas. 'Must have cost a few bob,' the prisoner would say, and would then ask about certain security procedures. These guys could easily find out where you lived, officers knew, and all the officers wanted was an easy life and a comfortable salary; the last thing they required was a return to the bad old days.

A gradual air of complacency pervaded the Maze. For instance, in his role as orderly, McFarlane would collect a bin outside the security gate and bring it back inside. Strictly speaking, this was always to be done accompanied by a warder but should the warders be busy, he would tell them that he would just nip out and be right back. Gradually, they became lax about accompanying him. After all, where could he be going? The IRA in H7 began to gain control over the run-of-the-mill aspects of prison life, such as education, the gym, football and the workshops, all the while gaining more freedom of movement and sussing out the layout details of the block. According to regulations, the only time a prisoner could leave his wing and go to the circle was to see the chief officer on duty, but this restriction was gradually worn down until the prison officers were acclimatised to the prisoners coming and going between the wings. Prisoners would make tea for warders and help answer their crosswords. First names were being used which further helped to undermine regimented rules. The prisoners were almost friendly, and the warders became psychologically conditioned to the new regime. The other republican blocks were mistrustful of this comfortable lifestyle in H7 and thought the inmates had abandoned their republican principles. But to McFarlane, Kelly and Storey, this was a means to an end.

As the escape idea developed, it was sent to GHQ of the IRA for approval and there it was given serious consideration. It required huge outside back-up and would be quite a drain on resources, conceivably being the biggest IRA operation ever. They would have to commit armed personnel as escorts for the escapees who had broken through, and safe houses would have to be secured. But for GHQ, the biggest issue was the hand-guns. The escape committee had asked for six shorts, which could be fatal, for if the escaping prisoners were discovered and the prisoners found to be armed, the authorities could then open fire, no questions asked. The IRA could lose valuable men. There was also the danger that some hothead could seek vengeance against a prison warder and blow one of them away, with dire consequences. Outweighing this, the movement stood to get some key operators back in circulation. Among the small clique in on the escape, there were some prisoners new to the blocks as well as the old hands. This helped the prisoners' cause, as there was recent acquaintance between GHQ staff and some of those on the escape. They trusted them.

Bobby Storey was a man GHQ knew to be a born leader. He had only been inside since June 1982, having been found guilty of weapons possession, for which he was serving an eighteen-year sentence. In England, he had been charged, along with Gerry Tuite (who had escaped from Brixton prison in December 1980), with conspiring to free Brian Keenan from Brixton in an elaborate getaway plan involving a hijacked helicopter. Although he was found not guilty, he was excluded from mainland UK in 1981. The IRA on the outside knew him to be meticulous enough to pull off an escape such as this one.

Aside from these practical considerations, the Provos had to consider the political implications. Although many of the concessions demanded by the hunger strikers had subsequently been granted quietly, the hunger strike was viewed by the larger public as a defeat for the prisoners. A successful prison break on this scale would be a huge propaganda coup. It was a big risk, but given the personnel involved it was deemed a risk worth taking. The guns would be made available and extensive back-up and getaway facilities would be on hand on the day of the escape. Word was smuggled into the prison of the Army Council's approval.

▲▲▲

Marley set about fine-tuning his plans. GHQ had sent a list of personnel whom they wanted on the escape, and he set about getting these men transferred to H7 without any notice being taken. Ironically, he was not going to be on the escape himself as he had only a couple of years left. The conditions sent from GHQ were that those who were chosen to attempt the escape had to have more than three years left to serve, and also had to be IRA volunteers as they could be either shot or conceivably charged with murder, given that firearms were involved. Two-thirds of the men finally chosen, in fact, were in on murder charges anyway and most were in their twenties. What had they got to lose? The timing of the escape was agreed. It had to be a Sunday as the blocks operated on a skeleton staff that day to lessen the crippling overtime bill. Also, it was not uncommon for the food lorry to leave the compound on weekends. Which Sunday? It was well known to the IRA that the RUC staged many roadblocks on All-Ireland Sunday, as it was the one day in the year you were sure to catch some of those IRA boys on the move. Sunday, 22 September, a week after the All-Ireland final, was chosen as security on the roads would be a little more relaxed.

There remained one small geographical problem: the brains of the operation were in H5 and the bones were in H7, nearly a mile away. Marley would have to find a means of getting his ideas up to H7, and he chose Robert 'Goose' Russell, who was stuck in H5 with a twenty-year sentence, as his courier. Marley would impart everything he knew about the escape plan to Goose who would then, somehow, get to H7 and join in on the escape. Getting him to H7 was the tricky bit, but Marley was sure that he'd think of something.

Classes started. Marley, armed with a felt-tip pen and a whiteboard, sketched out the escape route for Goose. He drew the various sentry posts, gates, administration areas, along with the various code words; for example, the 'Big T' was the Tally Lodge. The food lorry was referred to as the '*gluaisteán mór*' ('big car'). Irish words would always be used in describing the escape so as not to arouse suspicion as prisoners frequently learned Irish during their incarceration. Marley scribbled down the password for each gate, which changed on different days. 'Right now, Goose, your turn,' he'd then say, handing Goose the pen. Goose would start, but inevitably he would make a mistake, at which point Marley would rub the whole thing out. 'Wrong, start again!' It wasn't long before Goose's patience wore thin and he was ready to slap this wee devil, but eventually he got it to a fine art and could sketch the entire thing from memory on demand. Goose couldn't help wondering, however, what the point was in him having all this information in H5, when the escape was in H7. 'Don't worry,' Marley would say, 'we'll get you up, by hook or by crook.'

The prisoners were successfully dictating the atmosphere in H7, and security was as lax as it could feasibly be. That summer, there were no confrontations between prisoners and warders, as the prisoners were under orders not to provoke or retaliate. Bite your lip. One day, enjoying the new atmosphere, McFarlane asked the warder in the circle's control room if he wanted a cup of tea, as he was making a pot. He passed it through the grille to the grateful officer. Next time, he arrived with a slice of toast and the grille had to be opened to let this through. Gradually, on seeing him coming the grille would be opened in anticipation, a major security breach. The control room was supposed to be locked at all times. At other times, when McFarlane was sweeping the circle, he would tell the officer in the control room to get a coffee for himself while he swept it out, and he would be left alone in there to study the controls and how they functioned. The prisoners had the full trust of the officers and were almost considered part of the prison service, so much so that H7 became known among officers as 'the welfare block'.

In the end, the escape leaders in H7 had to curb the amount of movement between wings on the block as it had got out of hand. This caused no small amount of tension among their own ranks. To those ignorant of the pending escape, their leaders in the block were behaving totally irrationally. The others couldn't understand why they couldn't move about freely while those stopping them were ingratiating themselves with the warders. But this was a military operation and it required discipline and rules, which were strictly adhered to.

The take-over of the wing had now to be thoroughly planned in detail. Where were the alarm points? What guards were on duty and when? Which of the nerve centres could be taken by intimidation alone and which required guns or chisels? Who would be assigned the various duties? Those filling the various posts on the day were referred to in the planning simply as Volunteer A or Volunteer B, but as the day approached Gerry Kelly was assigned to fill in the actual names. In January 1972, Kelly had successfully escaped from St Patrick's, the prison for young offenders in Dublin. Whilst in Wormwood Scrubs prison in England, he was caught scaling the perimeter wall. As Kelly was a known 'schemer', constantly on the lookout for escape, it would not raise too many eyebrows to be approached by him. The operation needed to be kept extremely tight and people were initially approached in a circumspect manner. Who could be trusted to use the guns with restraint? Were some people in too long, and thus too out of practice, to handle a gun? A picture of who would be able to fill the various 'boots' in the operation was beginning to emerge.

BREAK-OUT!

Back in H5, Marley sent word to GHQ to send in the equipment. The authorities have never found out how these guns came into the prison, and it's still a closely guarded secret of the IRA's. They believe that this information could still be useful to them. These weapons were small hand-guns that could be broken down further for smuggling purposes. Prison officers speculated that they could have been smuggled into the prison in the vaginas of female visitors, as there was no metal detection of prisoners returning from visits. They could feasibly have been smuggled in by a suborned officer or on a transport vehicle. All we know for sure is that five shorts were sent in. When Marley finally had them in his cell, he looked at them and thought: This could really happen, we could pull this off.

The shorts arrived only twenty minutes before lock-up, so there was no time to dump them. They were still in the cell when, shortly after lock-up, an RUC man lifted the flap on Marley's cell door. What's the RUC doing in here, thought Marley, are we rumbled? He and his cellmates were all thinking of the extra sentence they would get for possession. How am I going to explain this to the wife? Marley wondered. The RUC officer burst through the door, saying: 'There's a twenty-four-hour strike by the warders, here's your dinner: burgers and chips.' After this close call the boys weren't very hungry, so the food was used to smuggle the equipment out of the cell to the quartermaster who stashed the guns.

Then word came in that the food lorry had broken down. The next day the plotters all looked out anxiously for the new food lorry and were shocked to see that it had an open back, with the contents visible to all. They wouldn't be able to conceal anybody in it. This moment of anxiety was short-lived though, as two days later the regular lorry had been repaired and was back in service. Another hitch gone.

▲▲▲

Many IRA men were in the blocks as a result of being testi-fied against in court by a former comrade. During the early eighties, a rot had set in amongst the Provos, especially in Belfast. Some volunteers had started to finger their comrades in exchange for immunity and a new life under a false name. They were the 'supergrasses'. It had a cumulative effect, for when one was fingered, he too started to name names and events. It proved a brilliant counter-terrorism weapon for the authorities, as it turned the enemy in on themselves, and made them paranoid. It was against this backdrop that the escape plans had to be kept as secret as possible, on the inside and on the outside.

The list of who was to go on the escape was being fine-tuned all the time, while being passed in and out of the prison from GHQ to the escape committee. But in H7, the net of who was in on the escape was widened out of neces-sity, and this meant that the security of the plan could be compromised. As more were included so too did the risk of 'loose talk' increase. Suspicion was rife. Storey was emphatic about the consequences of jeopardising this escape which, he reminded the others, had been six months in the plan-ning. If caught, they would be dealt with very severely. People were informed on a 'need to know' basis. Those vol-unteers who were involved on the day had to be briefed, especially those who were to be armed. Constant reiteration meant that their roles were drilled into them. They rehearsed every day. They had to be on top of the situation and react sensibly to all eventualities. They were reminded why they were using guns. There was no swim, tunnel or rope ladder. This was a take-over, and a mass break-out, a high-octane escape that required low-octane heads.

In H5, Marley had two further jobs to do, essentially courier jobs. The first was to get the guns up to H7. He sent a message to Storey saying, they'll be with you in twenty minutes, and true to his word they were delivered on time. As Marley sat in H5 waiting for word to come back, he listened out for alarms going off. But there were none, just a wee note from H7, which read succinctly: 'Nice one, boys.'

His second courier job was to get Goose Russell up to H7, and this required all his guile and cunning. He informed Goose that he would be going up on Monday, but didn't reveal how. In fact, Marley had asked to meet with the governor, a veteran who had risen from being a rank-and-file officer on the blocks, and knew Marley quite a long time. They met in his office. 'I need to talk to you,' said Marley. 'Talk away,' the governor said. It was customary for a prison officer to stand by at these meetings, so Marley asked could they talk in private. Uncharacteristically, the governor asked the officer to wait outside. 'What's the problem, Larry?' 'There's this fella, Goose – Robert Russell – a big lad on the block, who's causing terrible trouble,' explained Marley. 'There's another boy on the blocks and he says he's going to empty him, to stiff him. It's something that happened on the outside. I've said it to the OC on the wing and he can't control him either.' Cleverly, Marley then turned to walk out. 'What can I do?' the governor asked. Marley had the answer: 'Get him out of there. If anything happens on that wing, it'll be on your head,' and again, he turned to go. 'Where'll I put him?' asked the governor. Success! 'The only one I know who can control him is Marty McManus in H7.' It was no sooner said than done, and it wasn't long before Goose was in H7, with all the intelligence on what lay between H7 and the Big T, the Tally Lodge.

On the two Sundays prior to the escape day, those who were to take over the circle did a number of dry runs in order to fine-tune their timing. To this end, they had smuggled watches into the blocks and on both days everything went swimmingly. From the initial signal, the circle and the wings were to be taken over, and as each point fell, it was the cue for another point to be captured. Much to their dismay, two of the prisoners, Pickering and McMullan, who had been briefed for roles in the Big T on the day, were transferred out of the block. Then, days before the escape, Kieran Fleming from Derry, who was assigned one of the armed posts, fell playing soccer in the yard and smashed his wrist. He thus had to be removed from playing an armed role, though he was still in on the escape. The planners knew the operation heretofore was watertight, so whom could they get to replace him? Whom could they trust? They cast around for a substitute, using the same subtle vetting procedure, and the post was filled. Though they clearly needed six hand-guns to take over the block, the IRA had only managed to smuggle in five, so a replica gun was made, out of wood, by Gerard 'Blute' McDonnell, a dab hand at woodcraft. They had four .25s, a .22 and a wooden .32 gun, which they assigned to the least crucial of the six key points. The preparation could not be more exact. The worst part is always the waiting. Come-day, go-day, I wish to God it was Sunday.

▲▲▲

Early on 25 September, the dull morning sun cast its cold eye into the makeshift chapel as Mass was said for all the prisoners on C wing. There were 125 republican prisoners in H7, and twenty-four members of staff. Yet another dry run of the take-over was done to ensure that timing was spot on, and it was. The usual morning tasks were conducted without fuss, with all the enthusiasm of routine. McFarlane had collected the breakfasts and delivered them on his trolley to each of the wings. Along the way, he nonchalantly ascertained which officers were on duty that afternoon and reported back to Storey. Their sizes were set against those who were detailed to take over the Big T in officer's uniforms: they would have nine snugly fitting uniforms. He also found out who was working where on the day, and where the likely difficulties would be from the officers. Who among them was likely to fight back? One name, John Adams, stood out as somebody likely to resist. McFarlane had been told that he was on duty in the control room, the nerve centre of the block. This could be tricky but with sufficient attention to detail, it would be overcome.

Having lost Pickering and McMullan in the days approaching the escape, the plotters now felt secure that the personnel were in place, but nothing is ever certain in a prison context. That very morning, Robert 'Rab' Kerr, who was detailing the men who were to take over D wing, was called to Musgrave Park hospital for a routine operation for which he had been waiting over a year. Bad timing. He consulted with Storey, who told him to tell the officers that the operation had been cancelled, and there must have been some mistake. This refusal had to be gentle; if too forced, it would arouse suspicion. In the come-day, go-day routine of the blocks, his excuse was accepted without question. The last piece of housework to be attended to was the making of the ponchos to cover the disrobed officers. While Eddie O'Connor and Sean McGlinchey were engaged in this, the thirty-eighth escapee was invited to join the bid. He was Kevin Barry Artt, who was doing life and would hardly refuse. H7 was now poised for the operation.

▲▲▲

Outside the main entrance gate of the prison, an escort party of seven heavily armed IRA volunteers waited in the nearby loyalist area, Scarva, in a red and blue Ford van. Their assignment was to greet the escapees from the food lorry and escort them to south Armagh, where they would be billeted in ten pre-selected safe houses in the hotbed of Crossmaglen. This was the nearest thing the Provos had to a safe haven. Although there was a strong military presence in south Armagh, all British forces had to be transported there by helicopter and there were no ground forces at all. They were effectively confined to barracks. In the back of the waiting IRA van were mounted two Browning .50 heavy calibre guns, ready to blow away any would-be pursuer. The others in the van were armed to the back teeth, their weapons including an M60 machine-gun and an array of rifles. This was a major military operation, with the full backing of GHQ, and there would be no half-measures. The road to south

BREAK-OUT!

Armagh was interspersed with further armed IRA patrol cars to ensure safe passage. Once the food lorry had passed certain points on the road, three 1000lb landmines would be detonated on the road to prevent further pursuit. The outside help had dotted their i's and crossed their t's, and they sat back to wait.

▲▲▲

Shortly after 2.00pm the prisoners were tense with anticipation. McFarlane put fresh polish on the floors of both the governor's office and the welfare office to temporarily prevent their being occupied, as both contained alarms. The other seven prisoners assigned to take over the circle were poised to strike. Behind those in the circle, other prisoners were shadowing the officers and had surreptitiously obstructed their routes to the various alarms on the wings. They awaited the signal to overpower them. The very first step in the complicated seizure was for McFarlane to shout through both sets of wings for the 'bumper', the floor-polishing machine, but he had to wait for the changing of the guard at 2.30pm.

After a short delay the shout came. 'Where's the bumper?' he called, and the Provo prisoners were back on active service. Storey came out with the bumper and the occupation was put in motion like a ripple effect. As Tony McAllister took the canteen where four officers were drinking tea, Gerry Kelly moved to take the control room. As he passed the doorway, this was the signal for McFarlane to move to take the officer on the front door. McGlinchey took the officer that sat between A and B wing, while simultaneously at the other end of the block, Rab Kerr took the officer stationed between C and D wings. Storey was the spare man. His assignment was to sweep up the other rooms after helping Brendan Mead take the two men in the Principal Officer's office. When Storey arrived there, Mead was having trouble subduing Officers Smylie and George. Smylie managed to knock the gun away from Mead. It was only when Storey arrived, and put a gun to George's head, that Smylie finally gave up.

The nine other officers on the wings were then captured with chisels and hammers, and prevented from reaching the alarms. Prisoners brandishing hand-guns and screwdrivers overpowered the officers who controlled access from the wing to the circle. An officer in C wing was clubbed with a blow to the back of his head, while another in D wing was stabbed with a knife. None of the prisoners wanted to be the one to mess up the operation, so they were particularly ruthless in their efforts. All these officers were held at gunpoint, lying face down on the floor. Storey moved to take the medical room. He tried the door. It was locked, but he knew the medical officer was in there. 'I've cut my hand,' he said as panic rose within him. Why the delay? Was your man in there on the phone? When the key turned in the lock, Storey burst in the door screaming at the officer, asking him was he on the phone. He was re-assured. At this point, it appeared that the block had been securely colonised by the IRA. They ascertained how the various phases of the operation had gone. The shouts came back from the various wings: 'A wing, everything is ok, one injury.' 'C wing, 2 injuries, no medical attention required.' In all, six officers were injured in the take-over of the wings.

BREAK-OUT!

In the control room, the first phase of the operation seemed to have been achieved when Officer Doherty came out of the Men's toilet. The IRA volunteer left in charge of the control room moved to overpower him, and approached him, pointing the gun and shouting, 'Don't move, get on the ground or I'll blow your fucking head off.' The psychology of the escape was to use verbal aggression in order that physical aggression would not be required.

Whilst this was happening, Officer Adams in the control room spotted his chance to raise the alarm. He surreptitiously crawled towards the door, then slammed the control-room door shut with the prisoners on the outside, and sprang to his feet. Almost within arm's reach were the various alarms and phones that could scupper this escape attempt. He pressed his body against the door to hold it shut, and tried to lock it. But one of the IRA men saw what was happening: if Adams locked the door, the game was up. The IRA man put his shoulder to the door and it gave, slightly. He managed to force his gun through the space he had levered open, and fired twice. The shots reverberated around the corridors. Adams took a bullet in the eye and slumped to the ground, bleeding and unconscious. He was put on the medical futon bed, where the medical officer tried to revive him. He regained consciousness, but the medical officer was concerned that he would go into shock and needed to get to a hospital. The escapees were not going to weep too much over Adams, and he certainly wasn't going to scotch this escape. He was told that once the operation had reached a certain point he would get attention. The gunshots had had the effect of terrifying the other officers who were beginning to resist. They resisted no more. They now knew that this was a serious operation, with real guns that the IRA were not afraid to use. They had silencers too. All the officers were accounted for, bar one, but when Officer Leix came out of the Women's toilet there were no heroics and he was swiftly apprehended. Finally the block was secure. But had the gunshots been heard outside of H7?

All the officers were moved, on their hands and knees, to the two main classrooms, where they were kept on the floor with their hands tied behind their backs. Nine of them were stripped of their uniforms, and given ponchos and a pillow-case hood to wear instead. They were told to: 'Allow common sense to prevail. Do not be used as cannon fodder by the prison administration, nor the faceless bureaucrats at Stormont or Whitehall.' It was not something they needed to be told twice. The control room was ransacked for its prisoners' records, which were burnt in order to prevent swift identification and so that the authorities could not speedily publish photographs of the escapees on television bulletins.

The final position to be taken was the main gate to H7, which was manned by one officer. It was a familiar sight to see McFarlane sweeping the yard in front of H7, so the officer took no notice when he saw him approach, flanked by two prison officers. What he didn't realise was that the officers were, in fact, the prisoners McGlinchey and Hugh Corey. He too was swiftly captured.

▲▲▲

The plan was to drive the food lorry to the Tally Lodge, where eight prisoners in officer's uniform would take it over and subdue the officers there. Once it was secured, Harry

BREAK-OUT!

Murray and Goose Russell, dressed in uniforms, were to sit on the passenger seat of the lorry with three external security passes, with Gerry Kelly on the cab floor and the remaining thirty IRA men in the back. The lorry would then proceed past the British army base to the main entrance gate of the whole Maze complex, beyond which the outside help would be waiting. The other five – Dennis Cummings, Jimmy Burns, Eddie O'Connor, Brendan Mead and Rab Kerr – were to hold the Tally Lodge until the food lorry was clear of the external gate. This group was then to leave the jail in a car belonging to one of the officers back in H7, the keys of which were in their possession.

The IRA escapees now waited for their ticket to freedom, the food lorry. It was so quiet that McFarlane's footsteps echoed around the wings, but their minds were racing. They had shot a prison officer, which changed things utterly. There was no turning back. When the food lorry arrived, the driver, David McLaughlin, was captured and briefed for the mission. He was a prison officer, and the only one who could credibly drive through all the various security gates. He played a crucial role and had been identified as a potential weakness in the escape plan. He needed to be sufficiently scared not to attempt any funny business. Storey introduced him to Kelly, who was to accompany McLaughlin in the front of the cab. When briefing Kelly, Storey had told him not to talk to McLaughlin but simply to grunt in order to intimidate him. He told the driver that Kelly was a rabid IRA man serving numerous life sentences, and that he would blow your head off as soon as look at you. Kelly grunted on cue. Also in the lorry was Dessie Armstrong, an ODC (ordinary decent criminal) who worked as a kitchen orderly, who had to be in the cab so as not to arouse suspicion at the first security gate. He too was threatened, but he was a little more pliable as he was a nationalist.

They tied the driver's foot to the clutch, told him that a grenade was attached under his seat, and to copper-fasten his co-operation, Kelly, now in full officer regalia, was put lying down in the cab with a gun pointed at the man's crotch. There were to be no false turns, no signals to the other officers at the various gates. All those selected to go on the escape now made their way from their cells and clambered into the food lorry. There were hasty goodbyes. The rearguard would hold the block until it was safe to lock themselves back up in their cells, undetected. A call came through to the block and a warder was forced to answer it. Tummies were rumbling in the other blocks. 'Has the food lorry left H7 yet?' the warder was asked. 'Not long now,' came the reply. Loaded with its cargo of thirty-eight IRA men, nine of whom were in prison-officer uniform, the food lorry set off on its half-mile journey towards the Tally Lodge.

She meandered from H7 to the first gate. In the front with Kelly were the driver, McLaughlin, in his officer's uniform, and Armstrong, in his white kitchen uniform, both scared out of their wits as they approached the gate. There was a chance that the guard could search the back of the lorry, as they sometimes did. If this occurred, he was to be captured. Hugh Corey was to take his place at the airlock, hold the position as long as was necessary, then try and make his way back to H7 undetected. Needless to say, there had not been too many volunteers for this role. The lorry stopped. The thirty-seven in the back sat in darkness. What was keeping him? they wondered, straining to hear what was happening. The lorry was blithely waved through.

On its normal run, the lorry should then turn right to the kitchen, but instead it continued straight to the main administration gate. At this point Armstrong, the orderly, should not be in the cab, so he was pulled to the floor beside Kelly. Again, she was waved through, as it was not unusual for her to be used for 'homers'. Kelly donned his prison-officer hat, and sat up in the passenger seat while the lorry was parked in the van pool, which was beside the main gate at the Tally Lodge, the Big T. All the homework they had done on the layout of the prison had paid off up to now. So far so good, thought Kelly, his confidence rising. They had taken the block and now they were deep in the administration area, twenty yards from the perimeter wall, though still over a kilometre from the main entrance. Even if they were caught now, they had still achieved something.

There remained the biggest stumbling block of all, however, the Tally Lodge. The lodge had to be taken to execute the escape successfully. Kelly thumped the side of the lorry, and out sprang the eight IRA prisoners in officers' uniforms. It was here that Kelly was to be deprived of his real gun, which was to be used in the take-over of the Tally Lodge, and given the replica. Whilst Storey distracted the driver, Harry Murray switched guns with Kelly. They needed eight in uniform to take the lodge and Murray realised they were one short. 'Are there not supposed to be eight of us?' he asked Storey. Storey counted. There were eight. Murray counted a second time and again counted seven, until he realised that he had forgotten to count himself. It was a rush-of-blood thing. Leaving Kelly in the front of the lorry, the eight of them set off with firearms and chisels to take the Tally Lodge, where six officers were stationed, an easy task given their numerical advantage.

The officer guarding the first gate into the airlock was captured, and the lorry was admitted into the airlock between the two security gates. The injured and captured officers were to be locked in the transport office in the Tally Lodge. Officer Ferris was in charge of searching pedestrian officers coming and going from the Tally Lodge, and this position had to be taken. When he was confronted with a gun, he started to shout and run, trying to warn other officers, but was stabbed in the chest by an IRA man and dragged back to the transport office. Ferris had a history of heart trouble and died shortly afterwards.

Because the food lorry was late arriving at H7, the escape was about twenty minutes behind schedule now and its arrival coincided with the changing of the guard for the entire prison – not just one guard but over twenty, with a further twenty or more going off-duty. As the officers arrived at the gate for duty, they were admitted by an IRA man disguised as a warder, but once they got to the Tally Lodge, the escapees forced them, at gunpoint, to lie on the floor. The prisoners were hoping to capture all the officers until there was a break in the flow and they could continue to the main entrance gate as originally planned. It wouldn't be long, though, before their situation was getting untenable, as it became impossible to move about without clambering over officers. They had captured nearly forty by now and there were only a handful of prisoners brandishing guns.

Amidst this low-level panic among the escapees, the phone rang in the lodge. Calm was called for. Officer Wright was ordered to answer it, and told he would be shot if he gave the game away. The air in the lodge was electric with tension. He picked up the receiver, flanked by two armed and jumpy IRA men. On the other end was the Emergency Control Room (ECR). 'What's happening down there?' 'What do you mean?' replied Wright, tense but holding it together. 'Somebody pulled out an alarm.' 'Which one?' Wright asked. 'The one underneath the telly.' All eyes shot around to the television as the officers on the ground sidled away from it, like crabs. 'What'll I do?' demanded Wright. 'Just re-set it.' It was a simple matter of replacing the alarm, but Officer Wright thought this was a chance to signal to the ECR that there was a problem. 'How do I do that?' he asked. Storey grabbed his shirt and pushed the gun firmly up against him; he was skating on thin ice. 'Push it back in, you stupid bastard,' snapped the voice down the phone, and the ECR hung up. Wright was sure his number was up. 'Any more moves like that and you'll be in big trouble,' he was told.

Outside, Kelly sat with Officer McLaughlin in the front of the lorry. The lorry was deliberately parked in front of the Tally Lodge, in order to obscure the view of the lodge from the British army post about fifteen yards away. They were a tantalising ten yards from the outside if they changed plan and made a bolt for it through the fences instead of heading to the main entrance gate. Kelly's head was throbbing with nerves as he observed procedures in the lodge. He could see that a number of fights were breaking out. Kelly's eyes flashed from the army post to the lodge. What could be going through the soldier's head? More officers were arriving for duty. Things were going awry. The driver looked anxiously at Kelly. Storey had told him this guy was a homicidal maniac, and his main concern was that a real gun was pointing at him. He was nervous but didn't want to rattle this guy's cage. They were trying to keep each other calm, and a bizarre conversation ensued. 'Are you married?' asked Kelly, 'do you get decent wages?' 'Not enough, mate,' came the reply. Beside them, the mêlée intensified. Their conversation was interrupted by McFarlane, who arrived out to open the main hydraulic gate. In front of him, Kelly could now see a carpark, and open fields within a stone's throw. So close, yet so far. 'The balloon's up,' McFarlane said to Kelly as he passed. He wasn't sure what was going on in the lodge, but he knew it was bad.

The situation in the lodge had become impossible, and McFarlane and Storey conferred. They couldn't keep this amount of officers at bay any longer. They selected three volunteers – Kerr, Cummings and O'Connor – to stay and try to hold the position and prevent the alarm being raised, then ordered everybody else to board the lorry. One officer managed to bundle his IRA captor out the door of the transport office and phoned the emergency number. Another who approached from the back door saw that all was not as it should be in the lodge, and he blew his whistle to sound the alarm. Simultaneously, an officer arriving on duty recognised McFarlane on his way out to open the main gate and started to shout for assistance. Inside, Storey was overpowered and disarmed by the officers; this nightmare scenario had been overlooked in the planning. It was time to improvise. Storey surrendered, to buy just enough time to scarper. 'Okay, you have us,' he said, and then, in an instant, all the IRA men bolted.

Whistles blew. Kelly was still trying to figure out why the army post wasn't doing anything when two cars sped in front of the lorry to block its way. Knowing something was amiss, another officer seized the initiative and parked his own car across the entrance. He leapt out wielding a baton and said, 'We're going to sort this out and we'll start with you,' peering closely at Kelly in the cab, sizing him up. The passenger window was down. Kelly pulled his replica gun from under his coat. 'Fuck off or I'll blow your fucking head off.' The officer couldn't believe it. This was a take-over. He had to get assistance, and he ran towards the gate shouting up at the sentry post, 'They've got guns, they've got guns.'

The IRA boys had to move fast. The signal was given and the other twenty-nine prisoners started to pour out of the back of the lorry, like a human river. To the officers this looked like a volcano, spewing out a seemingly endless supply of IRA men. The magnitude of the escape bid was suddenly plain to see, as all thirty-eight escapees scrambled for freedom. The scene was chaotic as the sirens wailed a security alert. Prisoners and officers were in open combat. Storey, who'd been disarmed, fought off his captors and made a run for it. During this violent chaos, Kelly was in the vanguard, threatening the officers with his replica gun, repeating his mantra, 'Get back or I'll blow your fucking head off. ' As they retreated he dropped the gun to his side, terrified that the army post would see him armed and shoot him. To the soldier in the post, though, it was chaos, as some prisoners were in uniform and so all he could see were officers fighting other officers. Some of the officers were only arriving for work, and still in civilian clothing, so it was impossible to tell the villains of the piece.

The prisoners spilled out the main gate and into the carpark. There, six of the escapees approached a warder for his car. Knowing that an escape was on, Officer Gallagher threw his keys away. He was knocked to the ground and got a severe kicking. They retrieved the keys, jumped into the yellow car and sped down the kilometre towards the main entrance gate. Another warder, Officer McClure, witnessed this and leapt into his own car, speeding in the direction of the main entrance gate with lights flashing and horn blowing to warn the soldiers on the gate. At the main gate, the alarm was raised and Officer Talbot was locking it. The two cars were coming directly for him. He jumped out of the way. At the gate, Officer McClure swerved his red Skoda into the path of the yellow car to stop it. The yellow car smashed into the gate and jammed it open. Some of the prisoners vaulted the bonnet and took to the fields while Jimmy Donnelly was arrested in the car.

Back at the Tally Lodge, some were still fighting with the officers, while others had scarpered. As this wasn't in the script, nobody knew quite where to turn. Take a car? Half a mile away, you were into a British army camp. Go in the opposite direction? They saw Kelly clambering in the direction of the fields. He had been in this from the start, so it made sense to follow him.

Kelly had thrown away his officer's hat and the replica gun, and headed in the direction of the coiled barbed wire around the compound. This was regular wire, not the razor wire used inside the compound that would cut you to shreds. He decided that he would throw himself as deep into the wire as possible, and then clamber through the rest of it. Once in the coils he moved to get up again, only to discover that his comrades were trampling over him, using him as a human bridge over the barbed wire. As he lay there, cursing them, he recalled stories he had heard of trench warfare in the Great War where a soldier would be used as a bridge in this manner. Noble as this may have seemed to his comrades, this was not Kelly's intention. Finally he was helped to his feet and continued to race across the field. The prisoners couldn't understand why there was no shooting from the army post. They zig-zagged in any case, making themselves a difficult target. Fifty yards up this hill there was a ridge, behind which they would be out of shooting view, and they crossed it with relief. Meanwhile, the police and the army, with helicopters, were converging on HMP Maze.

It wasn't until then that they heard a gunshot from behind them. At this point, Harry Murray, Bobby Storey and Billy Gorman, a bit behind the others, were heading through the wire fencing when Gorman got snagged. In hot pursuit were a number of prison officers. Murray returned to help free Gorman. One of the prison officers pointed a gun at Murray, who returned the gesture. A Mexican stand-off ensued, with each ordering the other to drop his weapon. Murray shot the officer in the leg, and swung the gun to point it at the other warders. He then took to his heels, but was taken out by the British soldier in the sentry post, David Lee. He went down clutching his thigh. Shortly afterwards, he was brought to Lagan Valley hospital, where he lay on a stretcher alongside the officer he had just shot. They traded insults through grimaces of pain.

Bobby Storey, Sean McGlinchey, Peter Hamilton and Joe Simpson had made it through the fence and headed for a farmhouse. There wasn't a car in sight in the yard. They bolted across the fields towards the river Lagan, where they hid under the bank, breathing through the reeds to avoid being spotted by the helicopters hovering overhead. They were soon found by the RUC and military that were combing the area, and arrested after a meagre half-hour's taste of freedom.

Jimmy Burns, dressed in his prison officer's uniform, managed to hail a cab and asked to be taken to a hospital, saying his wife was critically ill. The obliging cabbie drove him past one RUC checkpoint, but at a second one he was asked for ID. When he told them it was in his other coat, he was duly arrested. Gary Roberts, who was on his own, stayed in hiding until that night, but when crossing a field he was picked up by a British army patrol. The authorities were slowly but surely hoovering up the escapees. Each of the small groups of escapees was unsure if the entire escape rested on their shoulders. Were they the only ones still free? Meanwhile the IRA boys waiting outside the prison in the van in Scarva listened to the radio commentary on their scanner and saw British army helicopters filling the sky. They left for south Armagh, believing that the escape had been foiled. By the end of that day, fifteen of the thirty-eight had been recaptured.

Over the ridge, the main body of escapees could see a farmyard, with the possibility of vehicles. They ran at top speed, and were thrilled to discover that the farmyard had three vehicles. The first was a blue Mark 1 Cortina. Beyond it, there was a Volkswagen van and a Mercedes saloon. Seamus Campbell leapt into the driving seat of the Cortina while another ten packed in beside him (Gerry Kelly, Kieran Fleming, Dermot Finnucane, Padraig McKearney, Tony Kelly, James Smyth, Gerard Fryers, Seamus Clarke, Patrick McIntyre, Hugh Corey). Seriously overloaded, she was coughing and spluttering down the lane, groaning under the weight, when they saw someone running behind them. 'Stop!' screamed somebody from the back seat, 'it's Goose Russell.' If this baby stopped, she clearly wouldn't get going again. Russell managed to gain on the car without her having to stop, and leapt in with his legs hanging out the window. They passed McFarlane in the drive and told him to hop in, but there simply wasn't room so he continued towards the farmyard. The remaining escapees burst into the farmhouse and demanded the keys to the other cars.

McFarlane and seven others (Gerry McDonnell, Seamus McElwaine, Jim Clarke, Terry Kirby, Paul Brennan, Tony McAllister and Dermot McNally) leapt into the Mercedes and took off. Meanwhile, Marcus Murray and Marty McManus arrived, took the last remaining vehicle, the Volkswagen van, and sped off. The blue Cortina built up a head of speed, ten miles per hour at least. They all knew about the security operation, called Operation Vesper, that would follow an escape from the Maze. Cordons would be thrown up in the area surrounding the prison, and so they had to gain distance, to get out of the secured zone. It wouldn't be long before these cars would be identified, and so they had to hijack new cars.

The Cortina crew tried to cut cars off on the road, but were in the wrong vehicle for that kind of stunt work. They came across a young trendy lad talking to two girls beside a modern sports car. Russell, in uniform, approached him, saying, 'I'm afraid I'm going to have to commandeer the car, son.' 'I know my rights,' the trendy replied, eager to impress his girlfriends. Russell shoved him aside, then tried to start the car, but couldn't. He had to ask the driver to start it for him. He obliged and then Russell, Campbell and Gerard Fryers sped off. As the car passed them, the others spotted the words 'turbo' emblazoned on its side. It looked like a better bet than their banger.

Murray and McManus, in the Volkswagen van, were picked up at an army roadblock on the A2, north of Banbridge, and handed over to the RUC. McFarlane and his gang in the Mercedes had managed to get about four miles of road behind them, but fearing that the sky would soon be filled with search helicopters looking for their bright green Merc, they made for a house they spotted in nearby Dromore. McFarlane entered the house to discover that the family that lived there shared his surname, though they were in fact Protestant. The escapees took over the house, and tried to assure its terrified occupants, two adults, two children and a young baby, that they would be on their way as soon as possible, McFarlane giving them his word that they would come to no harm. They managed to conceal the Mercedes by hiding it in the garage, and took up positions to the front and rear of the house, listening to news bulletins on the radio. As soon as night came they would have to get away from the house, but they knew that if they left the family by themselves, they'd phone the RUC.

One option was to leave an escapee behind, to hold the family hostage while the others made their getaway, and to send a car for him afterwards. Another was to take one of the sons with them in order to guarantee their co-operation. While they were mulling these choices over, another solution presented itself. The woman of the house struck a deal in order to protect her sons. Telling her IRA captors that the family were devout Christians, she agreed to swear on the holy Bible that she would not contact the RUC for seventy-two hours. Each member of the family gave their word to this effect and their captors agreed to the deal. The escapees commandeered a number of useful items, including a map and a compass as the two children were in the boy scouts. Prior to leaving the house, McFarlane wrote out an inventory of what they had taken, which he signed, and told them to take it to Sinn Féin headquarters in Belfast where they would be recompensed in full for what was taken. These were the actions of a man who knew that this hostage story would eventually come to light, and he wanted to be on his best behaviour.

At 10.30 that night, with their faces blackened, the eight escapees set off on foot for the border, moving furtively along country roads in single file. They slept by day, hidden in ditches, and moved stealthily by night, from nine in the evening until four in the morning. Led by Seamus McElwaine, who was accustomed to this terrain, progress was steady, and by Thursday morning, four days after the escape, they had reached the republican stronghold of south Armagh and safety.

Paul Kane and Brendan Mead, who had escaped in the car that had been wedged into the main gate, had to abandon another hijacked car and took to the fields. That night they slept under bushes until before dawn, when they set off again across bog-land hoping to reach a nationalist area. Exhausted, they reached a housing estate and saw, graffitied on a wall, the words 'Up the IRA'. 'That's us!' – they were in Castlewellan. They tried to contact local republicans, but as they approached a house they were spotted by RUC officers and arrested. Kevin Barry Artt made his way to Anderson-stown, in west Belfast, on a stolen bicycle, where he made contact with the IRA and disappeared into the city.

There were nine left in the blue Cortina as it struggled on the road south. Fifteen minutes was the most they could afford to spend in any one car before it could be readily identified from the air, and they desperately needed to find a new one. Despite having lost some of its load, this banger was still creaking under the weight of the nine passengers. The Cortina coughed again and it was clear that that was its last breath. It packed in on the side of the road, and there was no time to lose. Dermot Finnucane and Gerry Kelly went back towards a house they had just passed, to hijack their car. 'If we're not back in five minutes, you're on your own,' they told the others, who hid in the ditch. Kelly, still in his warder's uniform, consulted with Finnucane and they decided to approach the house under the ruse that they had been in a car accident. This charade was only half-formulated when a car approached over the brow of a hill. They saw an opportunity, but improvisation was required. Finnucane collapsed in a heap on the side of the road, while

BREAK-OUT!

Kelly in his bloodied shirt staggered about, feigning injury. He lurched towards the car and then he too collapsed on the road. The two-door Sunbeam Rapier, in which sat a husband and wife in their forties, stopped, then reversed to a safer distance of about fifty yards. Ahead of them they could see the Cortina, with all the doors flung open like an assassination scene from a movie, and a bloodied officer in uniform approaching them. Kelly had got to his feet again, pleading all the while for them to call an ambulance. He was getting closer to them. The man left the car and approached Kelly, trying to calm him down.

As soon as he was close enough, Kelly grabbed the woman in the driver's seat by the throat and told her not to move or he'd blow her head off. She was terrified out of her wits. Finnucane sprang into action. He shoved the man aside, ran to the car, and leapt into the driver's seat, then they sped the hundred yards or so to where the others lay in hiding. They beeped the horn and the hedge rustled with life. As the lads piled in, there was a distinct reluctance to get into the back as there were no doors. As more and more piled in the front, Kelly found himself gradually being forced out the sunroof. Finnucane put the foot down. As the escapees tried to settle into comfortable positions, Kelly found himself protruding from the sunroof from the waist up like a tank commander, with the wind in his hair, drinking in a view he had not seen for some time as they sped through the countryside. Up ahead he could see a petrol station and an opportunity to commandeer another car. He wriggled himself down to below roof level to minimise suspicion.

▲▲▲

Back in H7, the rearguard that had held the block secure began to hear of the ensuing chaos through the radios in the control room. They beat a hasty retreat into their cells, knowing that the RUC and army would shortly be on their way. They had swapped footwear and clothes amongst themselves so that the officers couldn't readily identify them during the takeover. In fact, none of them were subsequently identified. When the block was re-taken, the prison officers, in their ponchos, were led out and into a van, cursing and swearing vengeance. They were humiliated, frustrated and angry. The army and RUC approached H7 cautiously, fearing the prisoners were still armed, and every cell was thoroughly searched at this point. News came in that a prison officer had died, and the prisoners knew that they were in for a hiding. They thought that it was Officer Adams who had passed away.

That evening, the prison was gripped by terror. All the remaining prisoners in the block were moved to the empty H8 section, adjacent to H7, and made to run the gauntlet between prison officers with German Shepherds and batons. They were severely battered and bitten, as the officers goaded the dogs to attack on their long leads. The prison officers' pent-up frustrations were finally finding an outlet, and they went on the rampage. The innocent ODC orderly, Armstrong, was suspected of being an accomplice in the escape and was treated accordingly. He was beaten on the head and lost two teeth. The prisoners were refused medical or legal attention for ten days.

▲▲▲

BREAK-OUT!

A Fermanagh man who happened to be out for a leisurely drive on a Sunday afternoon noticed he was running low on juice and pulled into a garage. He was filling his car with petrol when a Sunbeam Rapier sped into the forecourt, with nine guys stuffed into the tiny car. Clowns! he thought. Then five of these tough-looking *hombres* sprang out and approached him. It slowly dawned on him that they were after his car, so he grabbed the keys from the ignition. These lunatics weren't too happy about this and they came at him, raining punches while trying to get the keys. He was a big lad and wasn't used to being on the receiving end of a hiding, so he punched back, giving as good as he was getting. These bastards weren't getting his car. He'd worked damn hard for it. One of them produced a prison officer's baton and started to lay into him, but he was punching all around him, like Popeye on spinach, keeping these vultures at bay. He wasn't going to surrender his car, and they weren't going to stop until they got the keys. The only thing for it was to throw the keys away, so he hurled them as far as he could into the long grass, where they wouldn't be able to retrieve them. The keys sailed over the heads of his assailants, and the fighting stopped. For the IRA boys it was hopeless. They all piled back into the Rapier, cursing this Leviathan of a man and, licking their wounds, they took to the road again. A short distance away, at a roundabout, there were two women sitting in a stationary car. Patrick McIntyre and three others took the car with what they thought was comparative ease, given their previous foiled attempt. The Rapier headed for Lurgan while McIntyre and his group sped off in the direction of Castlewellan, where two of them were re-arrested two days later, Hugh Corey and himself.

As the Rapier neared Lurgan, the boys were trying to distinguish between nationalist and unionist estates when Kieran Fleming spotted a sign for the Shankill estate which, its name notwithstanding, he knew to be nationalist. There was a shop at the mouth of the estate, which Padraig McKearney and Gerry Kelly entered. Behind the counter stood a teenage girl, wide-eyed. Greeting her in Irish, they asked her if she knew any of the Lurgan republicans they had known in prison. They kept listing names like talking address books, but she had never heard of any of them. Finally she said the name of an ex-prisoner on the estate, whom they knew. They asked her to take them around, explaining that they were in dire need of help. Although they spoke Irish, she was still suspicious of them. They could be a loyalist squad. She didn't know where he lived, honest.

A crowd of younger kids on bicycles had by now assembled and one of them said, 'That's my brother.' 'Will you take us around?' 'No problem, follow me.' The escapees were grateful that his security left a lot to be desired. The brother was watching 'Match of the Day' on the box when through the sitting-room door came a longhaired man, calling him by his prison nickname. He leapt from the sofa, full sure it was a loyalist assassination attempt. The escapees took over the house while their friend went in search of the OC of the area. They posted one escapee at the front of the house, one at the back and put the family upstairs. Those still in prison-officer uniform were able to don fresh clothes. After about twenty minutes the OC returned with options. They could all go together under floorboards in an old house, or they could be kept in separate houses, although with raiding parties some were sure to be captured. Unbelievably, the three who had commandeered the turbo, Seamus Campbell, Goose Russell and Gerard Fryers, had coincidentally arrived at the same shop and had been brought into the same estate.

They all decided to go together to the old house. A teenager was assigned to take them there, one by one, and he was the only one to know where they were. They lifted the floorboards in two rooms and holed up there for a fortnight, with barely enough room to lie down, until they were moved to safe houses across the border. All that was left for the OC was to throw the RUC off the scent. He now had two cars in the Lurgan area that were readily identifiable. The Rapier car he drove to Newry and abandoned, leaving the authorities to think that they had made it to the border. The second car, the Turbo, was one of very few in the country and far too identifiable. It was cut into pieces and buried, and has not resurfaced to this day.

▲▲▲

Of the thirty-eight escapees, nineteen remained at large for a significant amount of time. Three were later killed in encounters with the SAS: Kieran Fleming was drowned in 1984 in the river Bannagh after an SAS engagement, Seamus McElwaine was shot dead in 1986 and Padraig McKearney in 1987. By the end of the 1980s, a further eight were recaptured in the Republic, in Scotland and in the Netherlands. Kelly and McFarlane were recaptured when armed police swooped on their flat in Amsterdam. They were extradited after a protracted legal battle. Four of the escapees were recaptured in the USA in the early nineties and another was recaptured in the South. The remaining three – Seamus Campbell, Tony McAllister and Gerard John Fryers – evaded recapture.

In April 1988, after a trial lasting thirty-five days, sixteen prisoners were acquitted of the murder of Officer Ferris. The judge said that because of Ferris's history of heart problems, he could not be satisfied that the stabbing was the cause of his heart attack. No prisoner was ever charged for shooting Officer Adams, as eye-witnesses could not concur as to who had fired the shots. Twenty-two of the prisoners left in H7 shared a £35,000 compensation claim. In June 1991, the Belfast high court awarded £47,500 compensation to twelve of the recaptured prisoners for ill-treatment. For the prison service, this was a very dark episode.

The brains behind the operation, Larry Marley, continued to plot the means of executing another escape from the Maze. The IRA put a woman onto one of the officers, a renowned womaniser, in order to gain further information on the layout of the prison. Another officer who had detailed knowledge of the ECR was suborned, and fed Marley valuable information for his next, even more daring, escape plan. They were to neutralise the ECR and take over the entire prison. However, the officer confessed his treachery, security was stepped up, and Marley returned again to the drawing board. He was released from the blocks in 1985. Two years later, he was at home, in the Ardoyne area of Belfast, when a knock called him to the front door. He glanced through the window before opening it. The visitor wasn't who he said he was, and Marley moved to protect his family but as he did so, the UVF assassin fired through the door with an automatic pistol. Marley was shot several times in the chest, and died later in hospital. The IRA's greatest escapologist was slain.

APPENDIX
LIST OF ESCAPEES

Chapter 1:
Gunter Schutz
Jan Van Loon (caught on inside of wall)

Chapter 2:
Paddy Adams, Liam Perry, Dan McAllister, Albert Price, Hubert McInerney, Billy Graham, Harry O'Rawe, Chips McCusker, Brendan O'Boyle, Sean Hamill, Alfie White, Tom McArdle, Jimmy Trainor, Rocky Burns, Jimmy O'Hagan, Jimmy McGreevy, Jimmy McCann, Hugh Mór O'Neill, Kevin Kelly, Sean McArdle, Jimmy O'Rawe (unofficial)

Chapter 3:
Tucker Kane, Tommy Toland, Tommy Gorman, Jim Bryson, Sean Convery, Peter Rodgers, Martin Taylor

Chapter 4:
JB O'Hagan, Seamus Twomey, Kevin Mallon

Chapter 5:
Kenneth Littlejohn
Keith Littlejohn (caught on outside of wall)

BREAK-OUT!

Chapter 6:

The following 15 were caught in the vicinity of the prison:
Bobby Storey, Sean McGlinchey, Peter Hamilton, Joe Simpson, Harry Murray, Dennis Cummings, Billy Gorman, Jimmy Donnelly, Jimmy Burns, Gary Roberts, Marcus Murray, Martin McManus, Jim McCann, Eddie O'Connor, Robert Kerr.

The following 4 were still at large the following day:
Paul Kane, Brendan Mead, Patrick McIntyre, Hugh Corey.

The following 19 got clean away:
Brendan McFarlane, Gerry Kelly, James Smyth, Robert 'Goose' Russell, Seamus Clarke, Kieran Fleming, Dermot McNally, Dermot Finnucane, Tony McAllister, Seamus McElwaine, Seamus Campbell, Padraig McKearney, Tony Kelly, Gerard McDonnell, Terence Kirby, Paul Brennan, Kevin Barry Artt, Gerard John Fryers, James Clarke.

Three of the above were never recaptured:
Seamus Campbell, Tony McAllister, Gerard John Fryers.